Why is George Best a **pocket GIANT**?

Because he rose to stardom from a humble background.

Because he brought the Swinging Sixties on to the football pitch.

Because he remained an idol after he had walked away from his career, and even after his death.

Because he is arguably the best British footballer of all time.

JIM WHITE is a journalist and broadcaster on a number of subjects, including sport. He has written for the *Independent*, the *Guardian* and latterly the *Telegraph*. He is a regular contributor to BBC Radio 5's *Fighting Talk* and BBC Radio 4's *Saturday Review* and is frequently heard on TalkSport.

GEORGE
BEST

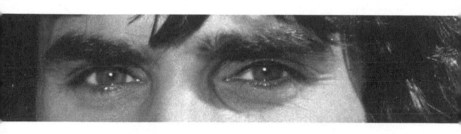

POCKET
GIANTS

JIM
WHITE

The History Press

Cover image: © Colorsport / Rex / Shutterstock

First published 2017

The History Press
The Mill, Brimscombe Port
Stroud, Gloucestershire, GL5 2QG
www.thehistorypress.co.uk

British Library Cataloguing in Publication Data.
A catalogue record for this book is available from the British Library.

ISBN 978 0 7509 8122 4

Typesetting and origination by The History Press
Printed and bound in Great Britain

Contents

Introduction

When I die and they lay me to rest
I'm going on the piss with Georgie Best

Chant sung to the tune of Norman Greenbaum's
'Spirit in the Sky' by Manchester United
supporters during a Premier League match
against Manchester City, Etihad Stadium,
Manchester, Sunday 20 March 2016.

It was no more than half an hour after he had staggered out on to the stage that George Best called Bobby Charlton a cunt. We had gathered in a small theatre in Richmond upon Thames one evening in 1993 for an audience with the greatest footballer Britain has ever produced and this was not what anyone had paid to hear. Best was onstage with his former Fulham teammate Rodney Marsh and things had got more than a little ragged. The star turn (though Rodney would probably remember the billing differently) had arrived late, his progress delayed by a diversion via what appeared to be several bars.

Marsh was there first, forty minutes after the advertised start time, doing his best to fill. Resplendent in a glittery dinner jacket and soft blond mullet, on his feet he wore shiny, low-cut slip-ons that barely covered his white towelling socks.

'Gout,' the man next to me said, pointing at the footwear, as Marsh struggled to hold the audience's attention. 'Those are the shoes of a man with gout.'

It was already shaping up into that kind of evening. But when Marsh was able – eventually – to pass on to the audience the news that the headline act was in the vicinity and summoned Best from the wings, there was a sizeable ovation. There may have been no more than 100 of the faithful gathered there to see the footballing giant speak, but the affection was obvious, mingled with relief that he had actually, finally, turned up. How we all wanted him to charm us, to tell us how it was, to throw in a few indiscretions, to be the Bestie of our imagination.

The visual signs, however, weren't encouraging. This was the man whose physical attributes were once so arresting he would invariably leave any room accompanied by the most beautiful woman in it. Now he didn't look good. The collar of his dinner jacket was flecked with dandruff, his face was bloated, his skin flaky, greying stubble was sprouting untamed from all parts of his face and neck. He stumbled across the stage to his seat, swaying, emitting a Tourette's-like series of grunts and grumbles.

The frame of mind he was in as he took his seat was horribly familiar to those who knew him. A hugely intelligent man, when afflicted by this sort of mood he became overwhelmed by a nihilistic sense of purposelessness. It had stalked him all his adult life. A few drinks were all it took for the questions to start filling his head. Why was he here? What was he doing sitting on stage in a poxy regional theatre spinning yarns to a few dozen sycophants? What was the point? He looked like someone who wanted to be somewhere, please God, anywhere, other than where he was. Even from the back of the auditorium you could see the dismay clouding those once sparkling blue eyes.

It was billed as a question and answer session and it soon became clear the questions for which the audience sought answers were not going to trouble the judges of the

Pulitzer Prize. Who was his toughest opponent? Who was the best player he had played with? What did he reckon to Paul Gascoigne, at the time the latest footballer to be dubbed the new George Best? And, talking of Gazza, if he were picking a first eleven of top footballing drinkers, who would be in it? Apart from himself, obviously.

This audience of men – we were all males occupying the auditorium – wanted to revel in the old days, the good times, those matches when we had gaped in wonder at Bestie's panache on a football field. All we needed was a line or two, thrown from the stage. Simple openings for a joke, these were easy questions to be soft-batted back whence they came with a smile. For a speaker mining the nostalgia circuit, it was the gentlest of audiences, the safest of open goals.

But Best was never one attracted by open goals. For him there was no challenge in easy. When he played football, if ever faced by an unguarded net, he would check back and mischievously find a defender to beat again, or the goalkeeper to taunt before slipping the ball past him. You can see it in the footage of the six goals he scored for Manchester United in an FA Cup tie against Northampton Town in the early spring of 1970. It remains a record individual goal tally in the competition, but he doesn't look happy about achieving it. As the count tots up, his shoulders sink, the celebrations become more muted. For his final goal, as he jinks his way round the goalkeeper, for a moment he stalls, stops on the spot, as if waiting for a show of resistance, as if hoping for a contest, as if rather insulted that it was all so routine. When he finally puts the ball in the net, rather than leaping in the air or embracing his colleagues, he grabs the goal post and nuts it, apparently angered by the ease of it all.

So it was in Richmond. You could see it on his face: what was the bloody point? He started by insulting the dress sense of a man sitting on the front row, asking him if he had nicked that suit out of a dead man's coffin. He then proceeded to mock the questioners, dismissing their queries with a sarcastic snort. He chuckled constantly to himself, finding his rude responses invariably hilarious. At least somebody did.

For a man who boasted an IQ of 154, this was not the brightest of demonstrations; his answers were by turns grumbly and mumbly. Never mind that his public had paid good money to spend time in his company; he showed little intention of delivering any return on their investment.

Sensing that his partner was in the sort of disruptive temper he had seen all too often, Marsh moved the agenda on. He called out from the wings the third speaker on the programme, the man who was meant to be a highlight of the evening's second half. It was Jack Charlton, England's World Cup-winning centre back, who in his retirement had mastered the art of crinkly anecdotage. If any man could haul things back on track, Marsh clearly thought, Jack could.

As the big fella walked out, grinning and waving to the audience, Best had found his challenge. Suddenly animated by the new arrival, he was the first to speak.

'I've gorra question Jack,' he slurred. For a moment, the audience was enthralled. What was he going to ask? Would it be a reminder of the kickings Charlton delivered in those hard-man battles that characterised meetings between his Leeds United and Best's Manchester United? Was it going to be a joke about the relative merits of Leeds's manager Don Revie and United's Matt Busby? Was he going to recall an international game between England and Northern Ireland, when Best's trickery had flummoxed the English defence and he had a perfectly legitimate goal disallowed after he had artfully kicked the ball out of Gordon Banks's hands and into the net?

It was none of those.

'Tell me this Jack,' said Best. 'Why is your brother such a cunt?'

Now this was properly shocking. Because it wasn't just anybody Best was slandering. This was Bobby Charlton, alongside Denis Law and Best himself one third of United's holy trinity of the 1960s, England's finest ever footballer and a man of irrefutable, unimpeachable integrity – the patron saint of the English game. The colour vacated Marsh's cheeks. Big Jack looked hurt. Best, though, apparently oblivious to the shuffling unease of his fellow speakers, or the silence thickening in the auditorium, seemed to think he was in possession of comedy gold.

'C'mon Jack,' he continued, giggling and snuffling. 'I know he's your kid and that, but you've gorra admit he's a cunt.'

It was at this point that Marsh intervened and declared the first half of the show over. We would reconvene after a short interval, he explained. Go get yourself a drink, he said. Not that his companion on stage needed any encouragement. He had already amply demonstrated that he was in a Father Jack mood: drink, girls, feck.

When everyone returned from the bar twenty minutes later, no one in the audience was surprised that it was just Marsh and Charlton who came back on stage. Best, we were told, had been taken ill. Yeah, right.

In 1993, that was what the world had come to expect when faced by George Best. This was only a year after he had appeared plastered on Terry Wogan's television chat show, sealing his place alongside Oliver Reed and Alex Higgins in the pantheon of the nation's drunks. It wasn't his prowess on a football field that was by then remembered, it was his fondness for the booze. When he pitched up on Mrs Merton's sofa in 1997, his facial tics twitching overtime, his habitual grunts and snuffles projected by the microphone on his lapel, he was asked by the spoof talk show host whether as a child he had ever dreamed of one day being known in every bar in Britain. He chortled politely. But, sharp as the barb was, it was no more than the recognised truth.

The irony was, he wasn't drunk with Mrs Merton. But then he wasn't always drunk in those days; it wasn't inevitable, he wasn't like that every time. When he was sober, he could be witty, engaging, thoughtful, exactly what his worshippers craved. But when in drink, spite and bile overwhelmed him. Riddled with self-loathing of his drunken self, he took out his frustration on those around him – his women, his son, anyone. This was a boozer who could pick a fight in an empty bar. And it happened often enough for notoriety to grow into expectation.

As I left the Richmond theatre later that night, after Marsh and Charlton had done their best to be convivial, I was walking behind a middle-aged man and his teenage son.

'And you say he was good?' the boy asked his father, finding it hard to reconcile his dad's claims of Best's footballing excellence with the shambolic display he had just witnessed.

'He wasn't just good,' the dad replied. 'He was the best there's ever been.'

And the thing is, despite a performance like that – despite his latter days on a football field when he became engaged in a spiralling downward trajectory of phoned-in cameos and insulting has-been exhibitions, despite the prison term, the bankruptcies, the tales of domestic abuse, the stories of bullying his only child, despite the insistent urge to run whenever confronted by responsibility, despite it all – the man was right. Best was great. He was a giant.

In his pomp as a footballer, shimmering across the turf in a swish of dynamism, bravery and panache, sending defenders the wrong way, scoring and making goals by the bucket-load, Best was unimaginably good. Better than good, he was sublime, an artist in studded boots, his grace and elegance gilding the game. When the mood took him, he could provoke a similar emotional response as a great piece of music or work of art might; he could lift the soul. In his teammate Paddy Crerand's evocative phrase, he left opposing defenders with twisted blood. To have seen him in action at his peak, when he was still fit, engaged and interested, performing as he was capable of performing, was to have been blessed.

At his finest, so good was he, so assiduously had he honed his natural excellence through practice, practice and more practice, that his manager Matt Busby reckoned him the most accomplished player in every position at Manchester United. Chuck him a pair of gloves, Busby said in 1967, and inevitably he would prove himself the finest goalkeeper in the squad. His name was no coincidence. As far as the British Isles is concerned, Best is the best there has ever been.

1

This Is Your Life

The problem with George was he never lasted
long enough.

Bobby Charlton

'In every era there is a genius. In our century a super genius came along,' Busby said, when Best was finally cornered by Eamonn Andrews and his big red book on the television show *This is Your Life* in 1970. 'He's got this appetite for the game. He's got a tremendous heart. Most important of all he has a great temperament. George Best is a football magician.'

And the magician bewitched a generation. Perhaps because of his flaws, because of the all too apparent evidence of emotional weakness that eventually brought him down, those of us who were inspired by his presence tried to forgive him every indiscretion, every howling embarrassment. This was not a superman, this was someone who, despite the anchor-like weight of his own shortcomings, made our hearts beat faster. That was why, when he died, the streets of Belfast were rammed for his funeral. That was why at Old Trafford on the tenth anniversary of his passing thousands of supporters held up their mobile phones with the flashlight on to celebrate a man who had illuminated their lives. A decade after he had gone, Best was still loved.

What was all the more remarkable about Best was that his light burned only too briefly. The glittering glory of his achievement was but temporary. From making his first team debut as a stick-thin 17-year-old in September 1963 to leaving Manchester United in New Year 1974, aged just 27 but already a withered shadow of his former self, his time as a footballing giant spanned no more than a decade.

'The problem with George was he never lasted long enough,' is how Bobby Charlton put it.

Yet in that ten-year glory, Best changed everything. It was not just his on-pitch ability that was revolutionary. His off-pitch image was something entirely new. Before Best, the professional footballer was the bloke next door, with his pipe and cardigan and his childhood sweetheart on his arm, a man already middle-aged. It was Best who attuned the game to a gathering appetite for youth, glamour and celebrity. It was Best, in his fashionably tailored clothes and luxurious hair, with a whirligig of photogenic beauties in the passenger seat of his E-Type, who first transformed the working man's pastime into Hollywood. It was Best who turned the footballer into a pop star.

But barely twenty years after he dazzled on the football pitch, there he was stumbling around on a provincial stage looking like a man seeking, with some intent, an early grave. It was an unedifying, desperate sight, the quantum opposite of his glorious peak. What was more remarkable in his post-playing slide, however, was that Best did not attempt to hide his fall; he sank in the full-beam glare of modern attention. This was not someone who went quietly. This was someone who did it on chat show and theatre stage, in tabloid headline and kiss-and-sell scoop, a man who shamelessly traded in the currency of prurience.

This was the man who, at the very last, sold to a national newspaper photographs from his deathbed.

Was what we had seen in Richmond a chimera, a parody, a mockery of the real thing? Or was it the other way round – were those moments of athletic glory just diversions from the relentless downward trajectory of his self-destruction? With George Best we have never quite worked it out.

Where did it all go wrong, George? It was the question that soundtracked Bestie's second career, the one that lasted three times as long as his spell as a top player, the one in which he made capital not from skill but from notoriety. We had heard the story often enough, told to Parky or Terry on the telly, told in a thousand provincial theatre appearances, told in the dozens of books he used to sell at those theatre events, at a premium price for a signed copy.

It concerned the little Irish waiter wheeling a trolley loaded with champagne and caviar to the luxury suite in a five-star hotel, where Best was entertaining some negligeed former Miss World, who lay amid copious casino winnings across the king size bed. 'Where did it all go wrong, George?' Except it had never happened. It was apocryphal. Best made the yarn up to mock the prevailing assumption that he was miserable in decline, to illustrate that he was, in fact, in his second incarnation, doing OK thanks. More than OK, actually. He was anxious we all knew he inhabited a world of ready glamour, easy girls and easy cash. He lived a life without restraint or responsibility, of a style that, if we were honest, most blokes would find enviable. Just as they had when he dazzled on a football pitch, the story suggested every man still wanted to be like Georgie Best.

Whenever he was challenged about his life, his line would be that he had no regrets. And why would he when he always travelled first class, staying in plush hotels and generally accompanied by a leggy beauty? Yet it was a strangely foundationless definition of the good life, this one he boasted of. It indicated a governing sense of transit, as if he were engaged on an endless search for something, somewhere, anything, anywhere better than this. As if he were trying to affect an escape from who he was and what he had become. As if he were ticking off the days in the lonely, soulless transience of airport lounge and hotel room waiting for the final checkout.

But then this was the truth about George Best: he was a man who spent more than thirty years in perpetual pursuit of the sort of fulfilment and purpose he briefly found on a football pitch. His tragedy was that he never located it.

Indeed if we were properly to identify where it all went wrong for George Best we can almost put a date on it. It was in May 1962. He was with the Manchester United youth team competing in a tournament in Switzerland. After signing as a 15 year old in 1961, he was living in club-approved digs run by Mary Fullaway in Aycliffe Avenue, Chorlton-cum-Hardy. Still an amateur, obliged to earn a crust as an errand boy with the Manchester Ship Canal Company, picking up no more than a few shillings a week, he had enough to spend on a Saturday night trip to the dancehall and maybe some chips on the way home.

Glamour had not yet attached itself to George Best. On this occasion, though, there was more than chips involved. After a game in which he – inevitably – scored the winning goal, he went out on the town to celebrate with a couple of his more worldly young teammates. These were two Manc street lads called Eddie Harrop and David Farrar, whose later footballing careers never warranted the attention of those compiling the record books. And they encouraged the shy ingénue from Northern Ireland to do something he had never done before: they urged him to try his first taste of alcohol. And his second. And his third and fourth. Then he lost count. He ended up that night carried by teammates back to the hotel, passed out on his bed, the room spinning around him.

For many a young lad that would mark no more than a rite of passage. Get pissed on your first big night and collapse. From there, most of that United youth team would have got cheerfully drunk on dozens of occasions without compromising their future well-being. But for Best it represented something different. Once it began he was gone. This boy, brought up in a Free Presbyterian household in east Belfast where booze played no part in domestic arrangements (though tragically that was to change after he had left home), was fatally undermined. He may have stalled the debilitating effects of drink long enough to establish himself as the finest player ever produced on these shores, but the moment he had given it access, his addictive instincts meant he could never shake free of its malign grip. That Swiss night out was effectively the signing of his death warrant.

Make no mistake about it, it was drink that destroyed George Best. It was drink that foreshortened his football career, ending it as it should have been reaching its apex. It was drink that turned his later years into an unedifying round of recrimination and embarrassment, of running from responsibility and hiding from consequence. In the end it was drink that took his life, furring up his arteries, corroding his liver, precipitating the comprehensive organ failure that killed him before he had reached the age of 60. No reading of the life of George Best can ignore this central truth about him: he was defined by his relationship with the bottle. 'Drink,' he wrote in *Blessed*, the best of his several autobiographies, 'is the only opponent I have never been able to beat.'

On the football field, though, at least when he first began, it was so very, very different. There he found fulfilment and justification. There he was happy and in control. There he didn't need to hide or run away or anaesthetise. He was absolutely right in his analysis: out on the football field there was not an opponent who stood a chance. There he was the king.

2

A Boy Who Knew How To Play

I think I've found you a genius.

Bob Bishop, writing to Sir Matt Busby

Best was born in the newly built Cregagh estate in east Belfast on 22 May 1946. His dad, Dickie, like most men thereabouts, was employed in the shipyards, an iron-turner at Harland & Wolff. Ann, his mother, worked in a cigarette factory. Dickie was softly spoken and kind-hearted, no bullying tyrant of working-class cliché. He ceded control of the family house on Burren Way to his wife, letting her take responsibility for the upbringing of their six children. She was the one who administered discipline when it was required. Dickie always took a back seat.

George was born in the middle, with two older sisters; three much, much younger siblings were to follow after he had left home. Dickie was a reasonable amateur footballer, but it was from his mother that George inherited the rarefied sporting genes. Ann was a more than useful hockey player, who loved the escape regular competition gave from the grind of factory and domestic work. As a young mum she continued to play and would take her children with her to matches. She noticed that George, from almost the moment he could walk, had a fixation with kicking balls around. She would leave him on the touchline when she played, knowing he would happily occupy himself for the entire hockey game just kicking, kicking, kicking. Once he showed an application, his paternal grandfather George Withers was the man who encouraged him, forever egging him on to kick and kick again.

Like his father shy to the point of being fearful in public, as he grew up the young George found comfort in his sport. Chasing a ball around the bomb sites and open spaces of east Belfast he wasn't required to talk. He could just play. And he did, constantly: after school, at weekends, all hours of the holidays. With no distractions, no telly in the house, playing football on the car-free streets was where he found life. If modern theorists suggest 10,000 hours of practice are required to produce a world-class sporting practitioner, Best had accumulated that by the time he was ten. Already, before he had left primary school, when he turned out for the Cregagh Boys Club side on a Saturday his ability was being recognised. 'We weren't that good a team,' recalls his old teammate Robin McCabe. 'But with Geordie in the side we always stood a chance against anyone.'

Best's obsession with football did not appear to have any harmful effect on his education – at least not initially. His final report from primary school was glowing. He scored 100 per cent in writing, 94 in spelling, 92 in reading. He had, according to the head teacher's comments, 'the neatest handwriting in the school'. In what would become something of an irony, his punctuality was reckoned 'v. good'.

Nobody was remotely surprised at the school that of all the pupils he was the only one to pass the eleven plus – the 'qually', as it was known locally, after its official title the

'Qualifying Examination'. So it was that aged 11 he headed off to Grosvenor High, one of Belfast's grammar schools, situated a fair hike from the Cregagh, requiring a daily walk across hostile Catholic territory. His parents were immensely proud that their 'wee boy' was going up in the world. And wee boy was an apt description: physically tiny, as he went off to his first day at the grammar he was swamped by his new blazer.

But at Grosvenor he encountered the first significant problem of his young life. And the way he dealt with it – or rather didn't deal with it – set a pattern for how he would cope with adversity throughout his life. Put simply, at the first hint of an issue, he ran away.

Grosvenor, in common with all of Northern Ireland's grammar schools, did not approve of football. The determination of the head teacher was to produce a side capable of excelling in the Ulster Schools' Cup, the annual rugby competition that has fostered the talent of many a future Ireland international. Rugby was everything at the school. Football, on the other hand, was banned, even in the playground, sneered upon as a pursuit of the lower classes, reckoned morally inferior to the egg-chasing game.

Despite his dancing feet and speed off the mark, the kind of attributes that would have made a formidable fly half, Best couldn't get on with rugby. And when he discovered that he was obliged to spend his Saturdays at school in rugby practice rather than turning out for Cregagh Boys' Club football team, he was plunged into an all-encompassing misery that compromised his approach to classwork. His report for his first term was filled with caustic observations like 'well below standard' and 'hard work needed'. The boy who had found everything at primary a breeze was struggling.

Not that anyone at home appreciated his distress. But then, why would they? Best told nobody, kept it to himself, bottled up his dissatisfaction, presenting to the family a breezy air as if nothing was wrong. But it was. Sinking into a downward spiral of unhappiness, he started to 'mitch off', as truanting was known locally. At first it was just the odd lesson and the odd day when he'd eat a bag of red sweets and persuade his mum he had a terrible raw sore throat. But it quickly escalated into systematic absenteeism. For much of his first year at secondary school he would head off from home after breakfast as if everything was fine, drop his school bag in the entrance area of the block of flats where his aunt lived on the other side of the Cregagh, then spend hours wandering around Belfast. At the end of the school day, he would pick up the bag and return home as if nothing was untoward, just in time to head out and play football until called in by his ma.

It was his older sister Carole who discovered his deceit, and informed their parents. Initially there was much tearful recrimination. But as it turned out, discovery was the best thing that could have happened. It was decided between the head teacher and his parents that he'd be better off leaving Grosvenor and enrolling instead at Lisnasharragh, the newly opened Secondary Modern school on the Cregagh, its intake almost 100 per cent Protestant. But it wasn't just that he was among his own people that made Best warm to the place, it wasn't just that he no longer had to walk to school past mocking Catholic kids: the good news was that they played football at Lisnasharragh.

This, though, was not an academic school. The expectation was that boy pupils would leave for a manual job, girls for work on the production line and an early marriage. Most of the jobs for the boys were in Harland and Wolff's yards, where the only qualification required was an uncle or cousin already on the pay roll. In a wretched indictment of an education system that wrote off pupils at the age of 11, the school (which closed down in 2008 following a steady fall in its roll) was in Best's day not allowed to offer any public examinations at all. Every child left at 15 without so much as a GCSE (or O level as they were known then) to their name. But, despite the fact he could do the classwork standing on his head, Best did not mind the lack of intellectual challenge; he could play football. Unlike his sporadic attendance at Grosvenor, he was there every day at Lisnasharragh, tearing around the playground during breaks, a ball inevitably at his feet. He was hugely popular with the head teacher Sam Barber, the rest of the staff and pupils alike. 'Bright', 'articulate', 'neat', 'well turned-out' were the phrases that littered his reports. He became a school prefect, the model pupil. More to the point, he broke all goal-scoring records for the school football team, dancing his way through opposing defences, his presence in the side making a backwater Secondary Modern for a time renowned across Belfast as the hotbed of footballing talent.

Through his school endeavours and playing for Cregagh Boys at the weekend, it was inevitable word would get out of the tiny magician on the wing. Glentoran, the east Belfast professional club, were the first to be alerted. At 14, he went for a trial at The Oval. But, in a move that echoed the EMI executive who turned down The Beatles, he was summarily rejected. He was, the Glentoran sages reckoned, too small to make a footballer.

One regular observer of Cregagh games, however, was less dismissive of Best's diminutive stature. Invariably to be found on the touchline in his long overcoat, collar and tie, Bob Bishop, Manchester United's representative in Belfast, was entranced by what he saw. From the second he clapped eyes on the dazzling talent on the wing, Bishop was convinced he was observing something special. This was a boy who knew how to play. Graceful, beautifully balanced, blessed with a sudden turn of pace, the lad had all the attributes that mark out the great. But it was Best's bravery that so impressed the old scout. Not just his physical bravery, that ability to face down a bruising from bigger, harder, brutish opponents time and again. But his moral bravery too, the way he would try things, the way he always wanted the ball, the way he refused to hide, even when the going got tough. On the pitch he seemed able to do precisely what he was unable to do off it: face up to responsibility. What appealed to the scout was that this was a player who rarely failed to apply the advantages of his skill – never mind that he was in danger of being blown away whenever the wind rose above the gentle. It was an attribute that meant he was surely destined for the top.

Bishop was unequivocal when he alerted United's manager Matt Busby, pleading with the great Scot to take a look at the prodigy from across the water. 'I think I've found you a genius,' he wrote in a letter that now has pride of place in the Old Trafford museum. And when, in the spring of 1961, United's chief scout Joe Armstrong journeyed to Belfast at Busby's insistence to check the lad out, he could only agree. This was something special.

3

First Team Regular

I played like I did on the street.

George Best

So it was that Best left behind the narrow confines of Cregagh ambition. He was never engaged at the Belfast printers' works where he had secured an apprenticeship. The moment he finished school in July 1961, he took the boat across the Irish Sea, heading to Manchester, waved off by his proud father and his tearful mother, who had bought him his first ever pair of long trousers for the journey. He was accompanied by Eric McMordie, another Belfast recruit who had been offered a two-week trial at Old Trafford. The pair of them were just 15.

His mum, as it turned out, need not worry about the length of their separation. It is fair to say Best and McMordie were not much impressed by what they encountered. Forty-eight hours after arriving in the grey, rainswept industrial murk of Manchester, the dirty old town, they were on the boat back. Best succumbed to homesickness and McMordie's moaning, and agreed to head back to Belfast and a life of easy conformity. He was doing what he would do for the rest of his life, addressing a problem by running from it.

Busby, though, was not having that. He wrote immediately to Dickie about the lad saying 'we'd love to have him back.' He didn't bother chasing after McMordie, who eventually headed to Middlesbrough. For those who were later transported by Best's genius, it was the most significant intervention of Busby's career. And when a couple of weeks later, after Dickie's entreaties, Best decided that yes, he would go back to Manchester, he found himself returning at a critical time in United history.

Busby had made his reputation by building teams on the foundation of home-reared youth. The Babes were his finest creation. But in the three years since that glorious side had been destroyed in the Munich air crash, the sticking-plaster squad that had replaced them had largely been made up of emergency transfer buys. In the summer of 1961, his health at last recovered from the crash and his energy restored, the manager was anxious to return to first principles. He was looking to make his side once more a product of the youth system (with the odd addition like the ferocious predator Denis Law, bought from Torino in the summer of 1962 for a record £115,000). And in Best he saw the foundation stone around which he could build another team of United graduates, players schooled in the Busby way.

Within a few months of arriving in Manchester, Best had been fast-tracked to train with the first team. Not that the methods he encountered there were any more sophisticated than he was used to on the Cregagh. United training in those days was an extension of street football. Under the guidance of Busby's Welsh assistant Jimmy Murphy, runs up the terracing, endless laps of the pitch and all-in games on the gravel car park behind the Stretford End were the things that constituted sessions. Best joined in with relish, applying his Cregagh street nous, playing like he had as a boy, ever keen to bamboozle his betters, to nutmeg established first teamers, to find articulation with the ball at his feet. And they toughened him up those sessions. Not least because Busby – for all his espousal of the more elegant aspects of the game – encouraged an uncompromising regime of physical contact in training. Often, under deliberate instruction from the coaches, the big men set out to bruise and batter the young Irishman. The harder they tried to down him, however, the more jubilantly Best danced away. The smile on Busby's face grew wider with every rubber-limbed escape.

It was, however, what Best did in his spare time that marked him out as something more than a mere prospect. He was forever searching for new avenues of self-improvement. He understood instinctively that excellence did not arrive solely by chance. After coming back to his digs from his tedious, pointless job on the docks, he would practise alone for hours. Out in the alleyway behind Mrs Fullaway's he would kick balls relentlessly at the wall. Once it got too dark to be outside, in the rooms he shared with other youth players like David Sadler, he attached a tennis ball on a rope to the doorframe. He would make sure it hung just out of reach. He would leap up time and again until he finally climbed high enough to apply his forehead to it. The moment he did so, the moment he succeeded in heading it, he adjusted the target so it was hanging higher, again tantalisingly beyond his reach. And so on he went, until he was soon able to jump above pit-prop titans like the United centre back Bill Foulkes to head the ball. Daily, he was putting deposits in the skill bank – deposits on which he would soon come to rely.

In those days, Best lived for football. And football was delighted to have him on board. At United, the word that there was a proper heir to the spirit of the Busby Babes quickly spread. This is what the supporters craved, the reconnection with the club's heart. Busby was looking to the future. And he saw the future personified in Best. Just after he had won his first trophy since Munich by securing the FA Cup in May 1963, the manager signed the lad up as a professional.

Then, on 14 September 1963, aged just 17, the slim-shouldered, jet-haired Irishman was given his first team debut against West Bromwich Albion at Old Trafford. He did not contribute the goal in a 1–0 victory, but Graham Williams, the Albion full back deputed to mark him, was so impressed by the maturity of his young opponent's performance that, so the story goes, he sought him out on the final whistle and said, 'Stand still son so I can have a look at your face. I've been looking at your backside all day disappearing up the touchline.'

Busby did not want to over-extend his young player, so dropped him back into the reserves after that one appearance. Exactly as the manager had hoped, Best did not take demotion lightly. Hurt by immediate devaluation, he upped his game in the reserves to the point he could no longer be ignored. Busby, smiling gently to himself at the success of his psychology, restored him to the first team for the Christmas fixture at Burnley. Dazzling in his vim and enthusiasm, Best scored in a 5–1 rout. His performance was simply extraordinary in its breadth and ambition.

However, Bobby Charlton, the Munich survivor and Busby's conscience on the pitch, was somewhat troubled by one aspect of what he encountered that day at Burnley's Turf Moor. For Charlton, Best's untameable exuberance had a not altogether attractive consequence:

John Angus [the Burnley full back deputed to mark Best that day] was a friend of mine. He came from the same part of the world as me and he was a tough lad, hard, brought up in a tough world. You didn't mess around with John. But George did. He humiliated him that day. He literally ended up without a clue how to stop him. I have to admit it was embarrassing to see a friend embarrassed like that. And George did that. He embarrassed people.

Busby too knew what he had seen. But he had a more ruthless attitude than Charlton, and he kept Best in the team, relishing the damage he might do to others' confidence. For those with an eye to history, one game in that season stood out. It was played on 18 January 1964 at the Hawthorns against West Bromwich Albion, the reverse fixture to Best's debut. And it was the first time Best, Law and Charlton played together. The hint of what was to come was immediately obvious: all three of them scored in a 4–1 win.

By the end of the 1963/64 season, Best was a first team regular, making twenty-six appearances, scoring six goals. United finished second in the First Division, four points behind Liverpool. But it was in the FA Cup that Best came closest to making an immediate mark on history. United, the then cup-holders, reached the semi-final, in which they were beaten by West Ham. Had they qualified for the final, Best would have become the youngest player ever to appear in the showcase event. Instead the accolade went that year to Howard Kendall of Preston North End who, by an odd coincidence, was born on the same day as Best.

Indeed, even as he secured his place in the first eleven, so young was Best he was still eligible to play in the FA Youth Cup, a competition Busby had long valued. That April he starred in the two-leg final against Swindon Town, scoring United's goal in the drawn first leg; the youth side went on to record a 5–2 aggregate score. Coached, as always, by Murphy, it was the sixth time United had won the Youth Cup. For Busby it was all the more meaningful as it was the first victory in that competition since Munich. Alongside Best in that triumphant side were David Sadler and Jonny Aston, two players who would share a much more significant glory four years later. United, it was increasingly evident, were back in every way.

If Charlton and a growing number of United supporters had noticed the force of nature suddenly blowing through their team, it was a game against Chelsea at Stamford Bridge the following season that first properly announced Best to the wider footballing world. Subsequently he would often shine at Chelsea, inspired by the swanky King's Road surrounds, applauded from the posh seats by the swanks drawn by the enveloping glamour that he had set in train. But that first time, as he drove his team to a 2–0 victory, he was absolutely, gloriously, stupendously good.

So good he was almost perfect. 'You could see in that game the complete range of his skills,' recalls Paddy Crerand, who played alongside him that September afternoon. 'He could do more things better than any other player I have ever seen.'

More things better: Best could dribble at pace, the ball apparently mesmerised by his control, then change direction on a sixpence, then jink, then check, then bedazzle. And he did it not once that west London day but dozens of times, demonstrating an insatiable appetite for the ball. At the end of his virtuoso turn, Best was afforded an accolade rare in football: he was applauded off the pitch by both sets of players and both sets of fans.

By now, with Best on fire, Busby began to believe he had the team he had been searching for post-Munich. In the April of that season, United were pursuing a treble. They were vying with Leeds for the First Division title and were in the semi-finals of both the FA and Inter-Cities Fairs Cups.

It was the year that the extravagant combination of sumptuous talent inherent in Busby's holy trinity of first teamers became fully apparent. Charlton missed only one league game and scored ten goals. Best, too, played in forty-one league fixtures, also scoring ten times. And the pair of them provided the assists for Law, whose twenty-eight goals in thirty-six league games won him the European Footballer of the Year title. They were the glittering, glorious bedrock of what was rapidly emerging as the most talented football team in the country. There was no more compelling entertainment on offer in the game than Law, Best and Charlton.

Yet, magnificent as Best was, Law, who in those early days invariably greeted his teammate when he arrived in the dressing room with a clip round the ear, noted a habit in Best he was anxious to see eradicated:

> Maybe he should have passed the ball earlier on. Maybe he was a little greedy. There were times when he'd have the ball, beat a defender and I'd feel I was in the perfect position to score and I'd be screaming, 'let's have that ball Bestie.' Instead he'd beat another man and another, just for the hell of it. Then he'd score. And you'd go: 'great goal, you greedy bastard.'

It was a failing the man himself recognised. 'When I got in the team I played like I did on the street, I didn't like to give the ball away, even to my own teammates,' Best once admitted. 'At times it would make them tear their hair out.'

Despite the coruscating firepower developing in the United ranks, the treble was not to be. Busby's side lost to Leeds in a brutal kickfest of a replayed FA Cup semi-final, in which Law, after engaging in countless skirmishes with Charlton's brother Jack, was photographed emerging from yet another barney with the shirt ripped from his back. They then lost to Ferencváros of Hungary in the Inter-Cities Fairs Cup semi, which, in the days before away goals counted double in the event of a tie, also went to a one-off replay.

But in Busby's mind, they won the one that mattered, the First Division title, gaining proper and immediate revenge for that cup defeat by pipping Leeds on goal average. It was the manager's first title since Munich. More importantly it meant, in those days when only champion clubs were invited to participate, that United were back in the European Cup competition – the pursuit of which had previously destroyed his finest creation. For Best, it was the competition that was to make him.

4

El Beatle

I caught a lot of damsels in distress rebounding off George.

Malcolm Wagner

It was one game in the spring of 1965 that changed his life. It was the game that launched him into an entirely new orbit, thrusting him into territory previously unexplored by any footballer. It was the game that announced him as a leading protagonist not just of football but also of popular culture. It was the game that made him a star.

United had progressed without much alarm through the early stages of the European Cup that season. They swished past the Finns HJK Helsinki in the first round (Best scored twice in a 6–0 home-leg thrashing), past Vorwarts Berlin in the second round, before being drawn against Benfica in the quarter final. The Portuguese champions were then true continental aristocracy, together with Internazionale and Milan, one of the few clubs to challenge Real Madrid's European Cup hegemony. They had won the trophy in successive seasons at the start of the decade, and in Eusebio they possessed the acknowledged prince of European football. After United emerged from the first leg at Old Trafford with a narrow 3–2 lead, Busby counselled restraint for the second. He knew the threat Benfica posed. He thought he understood European football. He was certain the lead was too precarious to allow ill-disciplined attack. Played in March in Portuguese spring warmth, he set up his side to contain, control, corral. Tactically what he wanted was to be thoroughly European. His final words as the players went out on to the Estadio da Luz pitch were not his usual suggestion that they enjoy themselves out there, but an insistence that they take care. 'Our plan was to be cautious,' Busby admitted after the game. 'But someone must have stuffed cotton wool in George's ears.'

Whether he had heard the instruction or not, Best was pathologically disinclined to conform to any restrictive game plan. When he played, he played like he had as a kid: without restraint. And so he did in Lisbon. Within thirteen minutes, attacking with reckless abandon, he had already scored twice. His astonishing turn inspired his teammates, who rattled in another three goals to record the finest victory by an English club yet in the competition. This was Benfica being torn apart on their own turf. This was the former champions losing 5–1 at home. Best's performance that night was extraordinary. The cheek, the devilment, the absolute certainty in his own ability was evident in every jink, every swerve, every dip of the shoulder. He eased away from the most violent tackles as if they were no more than mild irritation. 'George just went out and destroyed them,' said Busby. 'I ought to have shouted at him for not following instructions, but what could you say?'

The watching Portuguese could scarcely believe what they were seeing. One fan ran on to the pitch at full time seeking out Best, armed with a knife. He wasn't looking for revenge, he simply wanted a souvenir lock of his hair. Noting that floppy-fringed coiffure, noting that he too was a young working-class representative of a northern British town, one local reporter christened him El Beatle. It was the perfect soubriquet for the new phenomenon that emerged that evening. The Fifth Beatle: it was a nickname that rather appealed to the man himself.

But, good as it was, it wasn't just Best's football that caught the attention. On the morning of the game, walking down the beach in Cascais, where the United team were billeted, like many a young tourist Best had bought himself an oversized sombrero from a stallholder to remind himself of the trip. As United's chartered plane touched down at Manchester Airport on the team's return from Portugal, he put it on. The hat was a breezy, comical contrast to his fashionable knee-length leather coat. His laddish appearance was snapped up by the greedy lenses of the pressmen gathered at the airport to record the triumphal homecoming. Published the next morning, it was the picture that projected him from the back to the front pages. And no wonder – he looked great: handsome, smiling, carefree.

According to David Meek, the United correspondent of the *Manchester Evening News*, who was on the flight, his move into the centre of national conversation precipitated by the photo did not arrive by chance. Meek told him it was probably not a good idea to wear the hat with all the snappers around. Best, never a man to take advice, smiled and put it on anyway. Like his successor in the United number seven shirt, David Beckham, he had a natural instinct for publicity; he knew what would sell; he knew from the moment he stepped out from the plane in the hat that the pictures would be everywhere. It may have seemed counter-intuitive for a man who was so shy to seek out the flash of the camera bulb, but Meek says in those early days, Best relished the thought of fame, embraced it with real enthusiasm. What he wanted was to be talked about. Little did he realise, as he invited it eagerly into his life, how destructive celebrity would ultimately prove to be.

Given the magnitude of the football he had just delivered, it seems impossible now to look back and recall that on that night in Lisbon when he bestrode the footballing world George Best was but 19. Though United went on to lose in the semi-final to Partizan Belgrade (Best and Law missed both legs through injury) his showing in the quarter-final meant his fame was now unstoppable. He had already made an appearance as a guest in the *Top of the Pops* audience the previous year, jigging about unremarked upon as The Rolling Stones mimed their latest hit in a Manchester television studio, but this was now on another level altogether.

Like the Beatles, with whom he was invariably associated, it was soon apparent he appealed to everyone, across the age groups. Men – young and old alike – fantasised about being him, women – young and old alike – fantasised about being with him. Adolescent female screaming began to soundtrack matches in which he played. Girls wrote to him seeking – like that fan in Lisbon – a lock of the Best hair; if he did respond, it was generally with black tufts clipped from the Fullaway family's dog. He soon needed three secretaries to handle his fan mail. He was one of the first footballers to employ a commercial agent, and before long his income from outside activities outstripped his player's earnings. By the end of 1966 he was bringing in more than £1,000 a week, this in the days when the average cost of a house was £3,400. Everyone wanted a slice of him. He wrote ghosted columns for newspapers; he appeared in fashion shows; he was featured in glossy magazine photo spreads; he did a series of television commercials, bizarrely, for sausages. And in the spring of 1966 he opened the first of several fashion boutiques in Manchester. At that time everything he touched turned to gold.

And this was the mid Sixties, the very moment when growing affluence and a new social liberalism collided in a dazzling maelstrom of hedonistic opportunity. A red-blooded lad like Georgie was not about to turn it all down. The summer of 1966 was a busy one for English football. It was particularly busy for Best's teammates Bobby Charlton, Nobby Stiles and John Connelly, all drafted into England's World Cup squad. But while he was an established international, playing for Northern Ireland almost from the moment he was picked in the United first team as a raw 17-year-old, he was not involved in the competition that dominated the news agenda; much to his lasting disappointment, the Northern Irish team had not qualified for England's World Cup; nor would they qualify for anything while he was still likely to be picked. It was others that summer who would occupy the stage he was becoming used to dominating.

Instead, with a month off to be enjoyed at his leisure, with attention focussed elsewhere, he slipped off unnoticed for what would become a regular summer holiday jaunt to Majorca.

He went to the island, instructively, not with any of his teammates, but rather with a bunch of lads he had met in Manchester's burgeoning nightlife scene. The Best Set, as it became known, was not made up of the well-known or the famous but of young working-class blokes like him, taking advantage as the Sixties began finally to swing. It included: Danny Bursk, a fur trader, Malcolm Mooney who made his living in the rag trade, and Tony Marsh, a former MC for the Beatles. It also included Mike Summerbee, the Manchester City player and Best's one real chum in the game.

At the heart of the group was his biggest mate, Malcolm Wagner. The pair had first met in 1965 at Le Phonograph Discotheque in the city. Wagner owned a hairdressing salon, The Village, which was next door to the Best boutique. Waggy, as he was universally known (even to Busby), became over the next decade a combination of drinking buddy, stylist, agent, business partner, excuse-maker, confidante, firefighter and gleeful participant in a lengthening catalogue of alcohol-infused exploits. 'Mind, there were compensations,' says Waggy. 'I caught a lot of damsels in distress rebounding off George.'

The Village was an informal gathering place for Manchester's in-crowd and Best was frequently in there. Michael Parkinson – then working for Granada Television – was a regular and became enthralled by the Best Set. It was soon obvious Best preferred the company of people like Waggy and Parky to those with whom he played the game. In part, it was a generational thing. Footballers were expected to marry young and settle down; by their early twenties they all had prams in the hallway and socialised with the missus. But the life of domesticity in an executive cul-de-sac in the suburbs held no appeal to Bestie. He found little in common with Charlton, Law, Crerand and the rest, who would spend their Saturday nights out with their wives, doing nothing more daring than trying some white wine with their fish supper. While they wined and dined, Best was on the alert for action, wherever it might be. 'I got on with George all right, but we were different age groups,' recalls Charlton. 'He didn't listen to the right people. He listened to the wrong kinds.'

Right or wrong, Best soon found himself semi-detached from the rest of the team. In the dressing room he was a quiet, shy presence, sitting in the corner reading the paper or even – God forfend – a book. He found the company of other players – Summerbee apart – dull. Their joshing and banter was of limited appeal. And he baulked against the insularity of football. He still enjoyed its essential processes, the playing and the training, but he was growing weary of its self-aggrandising periphery. The last thing he wanted to do on a Saturday night out – or indeed, increasingly, on a Monday, Tuesday and Wednesday night out either – was be with his workmates.

Instead, away from the pitch he sought the company of Jack the Lads and spirited bad boys, night owls and drinkers. Single blokes like himself. Guys like Waggy who knew people like Louie Scavio, the main man in Manchester's notorious criminal Quality Street Gang. He used to go and watch Waggy and the Quality Street boys when they played Sunday morning football. And it was with Waggy and the lads that he would holiday in Majorca. He later said those month-long bacchanalia were the happiest times of his life. There – on a daily timetable which began no earlier than mid afternoon and finished at dawn – he could be carefree, detached, entirely hedonistic. There, in the days long before camera phones could communicate every last celebrity indiscretion on social media, for four glorious, sun-drenched, alcohol-infused, sex-filled weeks he escaped all responsibility.

When he came back from that first laugh-a-minute summer break to a country preening itself as home to the football world champions, he was not immediately ready to return to dull conformity. He started to spend more and more of his time at his boutique. Not because he was particularly enthralled by the minutiae of fashion, but because the lease included access to an upstairs flat. At the time, United's house rules insisted that unmarried players lived in approved digs and there was no way he could indulge his enthusiasms at Mrs Fullaway's. He regarded her as his Manchester mum, and he loved being mothered – loved the way she looked out for him, did his laundry, cooked for him, cossetted him. There was no way he would compromise their relationship by bringing home unscheduled house guests. So the flat was a godsend. It helped him hide who he was.

What he had discovered on Majorca's beaches and nightspots was that when it came to women, he was even better at the game than he was at football. He was a natural. Soon girls were turning up at the boutique in the hope of a first-hand encounter with the renowned owner. There he had no need for small talk, no need for dinner liaisons, no need for the politics of dating. They'd come in, he'd take them upstairs and shag them. He couldn't believe how easy it was. It soon turned into a game for him. He'd have bets with Waggy and the lads about how quickly he could talk a girl into bed. He'd set himself targets to see how many he could have in a day (his record was seven). He once charged Northern Ireland colleagues 50p each to hide in the wardrobe of his bedroom at the team hotel and watch him make out with a groupie. As business initiatives went, with that one he really needed to reconsider his pricing structure.

When it came to such encounters, speed was of the essence: the exit strategy the most important element of the arrangement. He described women to Waggy as boiled sweets: once you had unwrapped one you quickly just wanted another. And the more reckless he became, the longer the lines would grow, of those hoping they would be the one to tame him. None did; this was not a man anxious to embrace commitment. 'That was his biggest problem,' recalls Paddy Crerand with a smile, 'being too good-looking.'

Good-looking, but not macho. To his great personal advantage, Best's appeal absolutely tallied with the times. There was something vulnerable about his looks, something fragile and fractured. His arrival on the national consciousness and the Manchester nightlife circuit coincided with a growing fashion in movies and pop music for a more feminised masculinity; he fitted perfectly into that slimline, snake-hipped era of Terence Stamp, David Hemmings and Mick Jagger.

With his long hair, tight tops and extravagant trousers he predated David Bowie's androgyny by a good five years. Unlike Bowie, though, there was nothing remotely gender bending about him. It was women he attracted. Which was a happy coincidence because he rather enjoyed their interest. But though he excited the new generation of teenyboppers, Best found himself emotionally drawn to older women. In those early days, when he was barely out of his teens, he had several liaisons with women in their late twenties and early thirties, several of them married, women who found his boyish insouciance irresistible, women who could mother him. He once told Michael Parkinson that he never turned anyone down. If a woman was kind enough to give herself to him, who was he to refuse to be accommodating? He was not fussy or picky, just accumulative. And the list of encounters grew exponentially. The academic and feminist Germaine Greer, seven years his senior and then a researcher at Granada, recalls Best as being, physically, the most stunning man she had met. It was all in his eyes, she reckons: one glance had the ability to weaken the most resolute of female knees at a distance of fifty feet. When he entered a room, she says, every woman in it immediately wanted to bed him. 'He was the focus of attention,' she once told me. 'You could not take your eyes off him.' Waggy was equally smitten. 'He was gorgeous, absolutely stunning,' says Best's court jester, 'and, despite being a hairdresser, I'm not gay.'

Back in Aycliff Avenue, where Best would return for ever more fleeting visits, often arriving with the milkman and slipping into his room just before breakfast, Mrs Fullaway noticed a growing sophistication in her tenant. His landlady put it down to all that Continental cuisine he was getting on European trips with United, as she related when Best appeared on *This is Your Life*:

> All of a sudden he was a bit of a gourmet. From fish and chips he suddenly decided he liked steak Diane. He took me to a restaurant to show me how it was cooked. I had a go at it. I poured brandy on the steak, stuck it in the oven and hoped for the best.

In the autumn of 1966, even on Mrs Fullaway's kitchen table the old world and the new were in gathering opposition. The time of post-war frugality and gabardine-clad conformity was being overwhelmed by the headlong dash into wealth, fame and the solipsistic pursuit of the good time. And George Best found himself at the heart of the conflict. This was unexplored territory for a sportsman and he had no one to help him plot a route. Busby was simply bemused by the pace and speed of it all. United's manager understood a pre-war world of deference, of the maximum wage, of players turning middle-aged before they were 25. He didn't understand Georgie Best, this one-man wrecking ball to convention.

Even among his contemporaries in the dressing room Best was an oddity, a one-off. Charlton stood by, aloof. Law and Crerand thought it none of their business to advise their young teammate. Besides, they had their own game and their own families to look out for. Aston, Sadler and the other young players had steady girls, soon to be fiancées. They didn't want to jeopardise their relationships by cavorting with Bestie. They weren't even sure they wanted to introduce him to their other halves. They didn't want to tempt fate. It meant, as he circumnavigated Planet Fame, Bestie did so without a guiding hand to steady his orbit. He was on his own as a new order formed around his magical feet.

Not that anyone would have appreciated there was an issue, watching him back then on the football field.

5

Gloriously Unstoppable

It was showbusiness as far as I was concerned.

George Best

That season, 1966/67, Best was gloriously unstoppable, a whirlwind of talent. Like Bobby Charlton, he played in every league game for United, a constant presence, tormenting opponents with his blithe diffidence. As they won the First Division title, his charisma gave his side an urgency, a gusto, a vivacious sense of adventure. This was not a league victory achieved by the pragmatic embrace of attrition. It was one attained by the simple tactical expedient of scoring more goals than the opposition.

The intent was there from their opening game, in which they beat West Bromwich Albion 5–3, with Law and Best both scoring. And it continued through the year, right up to the game in which they secured the title, the penultimate fixture of the season, away at West Ham. The Hammers were a side that included a golden trinity of their own, three of the England team that had just won the World Cup. But the presence of Martin Peters, Geoff Hurst and the incomparable Bobby Moore (not to mention a 20-year-old Harry Redknapp playing on the wing) offered little in the way of intimidation for Best, Law and Charlton. In those days when a victory yielded only two points and the abiding assumption was that champions were made by winning at home and drawing away, United needed only to accrue a point to seal the championship from Nottingham Forest. But rather than going out in the East End to contain, to be cagey, to settle for a draw, the spirit of that Benfica game infected the visitors' dressing room. That was how Best saw football: not as a demonstration of tactical know-how, a chess match played on grass, but as fun. 'I considered myself an entertainer,' he said of his approach. 'It was showbusiness as far as I was concerned.' His attitude was infectious. Taking their lead from the showman alongside them, United were 3–0 up after twenty minutes that April day in the East End. At half-time, alarmed by the ease of it all, Busby issued his instruction: '3–0's a bit dodgy. Keep it tight.' No one was listening.

'We scored straight from the kick off,' recalls Crerand of the second half. 'And Matt, God bless him, came out a minute later, saw West Ham kicking off and thought it was the start of the game. 'Boss, it's 4–0,' we said. So he said "Och, go out and attack them, then."'

United did just that, eventually winning 6–1, with all three of their golden trinity on the scoresheet. The result provoked a mass pitch invasion from the huge contingent of United supporters who had gathered in the East End.

'Upton Park was bedlam,' wrote David Meek in the *Manchester Evening News*:

All hell was breaking loose as United were being roared on by over 30,000 near hysterical supporters. The referee had ordered the ball boys to try and clear the goalmouth which was knee deep in toilet rolls. The St John ambulance men were streaming along the sides of the pitch, their stretchers laden with fans who had succumbed to hysteria.

They were not simply being felled by hysteria. Outside the stadium after the game, the ugly fighting between the two sets of supporters was a harbinger of a coming era of more robust football fandom.

But on the pitch, as United seized their second title in three seasons, Best loved every minute of it: the tension, the aggression, the catharsis of victory. He went out into London after the game and celebrated by doing what was by now becoming a habit: he got bladdered.

No one saw it as an issue that night. Just as they didn't when he toasted the end of the Home International championships in which he single-handedly beat Scotland in a quite extraordinary performance for Northern Ireland. Just as they didn't as he headed off to Majorca that June for another indulgent month of boozing and birding it. He was 21 years old, he was wealthy beyond the dreams of Croesus and he had just won the football league: how else was he going to enjoy himself?

Closer inspection, however, would demonstrate a less benevolent truth: for George Best booze was no longer something to mark high days and holidays. It was becoming woven into the fabric of his daily life. When the new season started, in the evenings, after training, Best no longer addressed a tennis ball hanging from Mrs Fullaway's doorframe. He no longer found an appeal in whiling away his down time at the snooker club. He was out with the lads, drinking. Or increasingly he was out on his own, seeking some escape from the ever-present, ever-encroaching talons of celebrity.

His search for solitude was understandable, because wherever he went, he was the centre of attraction. He didn't ask for it, it was just that it was drawn to him; he acted as an attention magnet. Sure, it might have helped if he hadn't bought a string of luridly coloured fancy-dan motors, Lotus Elans and E-Types that he routinely drove too fast. As he accumulated speeding tickets, he inevitably got himself banned from driving. Soon he was obliged to hire a chauffeur to ferry him to training. After training, he'd head off in whatever motor he had in search of a good time. It would often turn into a long night for his driver, obliged to hang around as Best patrolled Manchester's nightspots.

As he made his rounds, the Best Set was expanding. The entertainer Kenny Lynch would join up when he was in town. Parky was there too, as was the barrister George Carmen. And John Birt, the future Director General of the BBC, then a producer at Granada. And Best was the epicentre of it all. It meant he was rarely on his own. In public he found himself surrounded, prodded and poked. He had on his arm the pick of models and actresses, the best-looking women in town and beyond. Though once he selected a date from the lengthening line of those demanding his attention, he found it hard to be faithful for more than a few hours. Temptation always beckoned. There was always another woman looking for his acquaintance. Commitment, like responsibility was something to be avoided at all costs. Not least responsibility to his family back home in Belfast.

Though generous financially, Best was parsimonious with his time. His trips to see Dickie and Ann, his older sisters, his young twin siblings and his baby brother became rarer than drink-free nights. He was never there at Christmas – he was playing. In the summer, he was in Majorca. Even when he headed back to Northern Ireland for a Home International he would steer clear of Burren Way, citing time commitments, later using the Troubles as an excuse, claiming he did not want to draw possibly murderous attention to his loved ones. The truth was he found his visits back home, and the round of relatives and friends lining up to look at him, to touch him, to ruffle his hair, a bore. He had other things to do, other places to be. He needed to be somewhere else. It didn't matter where.

For Ann, the strain brought on by the emotional distance from her precious Geordie was becoming intolerable. The contact was minimal. He never called, and when she tried to call him, he was never there. There was a drift of notes pushed under his door by Mrs Fullaway. Months would pass without word, her only news of her boy what she picked up from the papers. There was a lot of that, mind. Initially she relished the novelty of vicarious fame, of being pointed at in the street, of being congratulated for being wee Geordie's ma. But as he became public property, she shied away, bristling with the embarrassment as the headlines became more lurid, as the tales became more exaggerated, wondering why her boy had left her to face the consequence of his renown without ever actually deigning to see her.

After taking her first drink at the age of 44, she rapidly sought solace in the bottle. Like her son, she was not a happy drunk. Bitter, angry and abandoned she was clearly in trouble. Not that Best noticed. He was on the other side of the Irish Sea, having the time of his and several others' lives. As Ann's drinking became more of a problem, as Belfast became simultaneously a more dangerous, sectarian place, it was clear that what he should have done was to intervene, bring his folks to live near him in Manchester and set them up in style in Bowdon or Didsbury, close at hand, getting them away from the Troubles and allowing them to engage directly with his fame. But in a manner that was clearly genetic, Ann kept quiet about her decline. The last thing she wanted was for her wonderful George to see her like that. On the rare occasions he showed up, she made sure she was sober. Even had he bothered to look, even had he bothered to ask, Best would not have been made aware there was an issue. Everything, as it always was in the Best world, was brushed under the carpet.

Yet as he grew ever less assiduous, ever less professional, still the residue of his early training regime lingered. 1967/68 was Best's *annus mirabilis*. On the pitch he was simply untouchable, adding a sheen of experience to his innate zest, now better able to pick a pass, to judge the pace of a defender. Even as his enthusiasm for training was waning, his instincts kept him one step ahead of those who sought to control him through aggression. And how they tried. In those days aggression in football was institutionally condoned. This was a man's game and it was reckoned by the presiding authorities that men should be able to take an assault on their shins without complaint. Best was subject to routine aggression. There was nothing light-touch about it, either; it was was full-on and brutal. Full backs tried to check him by swishing his ankles from under him. Defenders would attempt on-pitch surgery on his tendons without the benefit of anaesthetic. He would return to the dressing room after a game with sufficient wounds to compile a medical encyclopaedia. *The Sunday Times* ran a picture of him after one game that season, standing in the dressing room, wearing only his shorts, the blood dribbling down his shins from the open gashes, his skin blotched with bruising, pockmarked with the consequences of his excellence. He was, in every sense, a marked man.

The thing was, despite the aggression, he still kept one step ahead of the chasing pack. He was too quick for them, too agile, too lithe, too cunning. There is footage of Chelsea's Ron Harris living up to his Chopper soubriquet in the Old Trafford mud one game that epitomises that methodology. As his opponent slaloms towards goal, Harris launches himself at Best's legs. This was less a tackle more an attempt at actual bodily harm. As he flies in, Best sways slightly, moving instinctively away from the arc of assault, freeing himself to speed on towards the goal. As Harris slides off across the mud somewhere towards Stretford, Best barely wobbles – and goes on to score.

Time and again it happened. But Best was so good no one could apply the telling blow; kicks, punches, spittle and head butts were flung at him, but he was never slowed.

Despite being subject to regular onslaught, he played in every league game that term, scoring twenty-four goals, an eye-watering return for a winger. The truth was, he made the game look easy. As a growing body of chroniclers were eager to note. 'His game is an amalgam of superb, almost supernatural balance, unbreakable spirit, a delicacy of touch that stays true no matter how fast he moves, limitless ingenuity and ambition, and force out of all proportion to his physique,' wrote the great newspaperman Hugh McIlvanney, who was increasingly drawn to report on Best's coruscating performances. 'He carries on to the field a constant threat of the impossible.'

Nice as such analysis was, Best didn't need to be told. He knew what he was. It was the same in training. The gilded occupants of the United dressing room found it no easier to stop him than their opponents. On the club's newly acquired Cliff training pitch, he kept the ball for so long that Jimmy Murphy introduced two-touch football, just to provide some sort of requirement on him to pass. Two touches and you were obliged to give the ball away. Best took one touch, then played the ball against the shins of an opponent, taking the return and setting himself up for another two. So Murphy introduced one-touch football. Again, he played the first touch against the teammate's legs, took the rebound and, like a pinball wizard, cannoned his way through the defence to goal, engaging in a one-touch dribble, refusing to yield to Murphy's exasperated instruction that he just pass the bloody thing. Every time he did it, the scale of the challenge diminished. This football lark, it was all becoming a bit of an open goal.

So it was that watching him in action on the pitch it was impossible to believe anything was remotely untoward in Best's life. Busby, for one, was entirely taken in by Best's subterfuge, by the fact that a night out for the player would usually start at the restaurant where the manager was dining with his wife, drink a coke and claim when he left that he was heading back to Mrs Fullaway's for an early night.

6

The Greatest Day

It was the beginning of the end.

George Best

It was impossible to see beyond the splendour of his performances, as they drove United that term to the ultimate platform: the European Cup final. He scored in the second round against Hibernian; he scored the only goal in the first leg of the semi against Madrid; in every round, his jinking runs confounded every opponent. His performance was routinely match winning. That season Best was joint leading scorer in the English league, with twenty-eight goals (and four more in other competitions). He was hotter than Dubai.

Best himself became convinced there was something more than mere performance – even performance as good as his – that carried his side to the grandest of all club matches, played at Wembley in the spring of 1968. His affection for his manager absolute, total and unyielding, Best came to believe that the team – him included – were taken to the final borne on a riptide of emotion. Ten years on from Munich, with the manager ageing rapidly before their eyes, exhausted by the ceaseless round of the football calendar, there was a view in the dressing room that this was the last chance they had to do it for him. They recalled the bitter tears he had shed in the dressing room after they had failed against Partizan Belgrade two years before, when he appeared convinced he would never now make the final. There was an unspoken agreement among the senior players that they had to do whatever was necessary to allow the Boss finally to fulfil the destiny he had set out to achieve with his Babes. They knew that was the only way he could begin to reconcile their death. That way catharsis lay. And once that unspoken decision had been made, fate seemed to take over.

There was no doubt about Best's affection for Busby. It went way beyond mere respect. He loved the man. He recalled that Busby had a face that seemed to light up a room, like the pictures of saints he had seen in his school books. He would do anything to please him. Well, anything except effect proper change in his lifestyle. He always told the Boss during their increasingly frequent disciplinary meetings in the office that he was determined to sort himself out – even when he knew he had no such intention.

The depth of his affection gave impetus to his performances that season. And when, largely thanks to Best's unceasing efforts, United eased past Real Madrid in the European Cup semi-final, he remembered that Busby's face was not so much glowing, it was on fire, ablaze. Everything he had set out to do was now within reach. That the goal which took them to the final was scored in the elevated surrounds of the Santiago Bernabéu stadium by Bill Foulkes, the foresquare centre back who had walked uninjured from the plane wreckage on the Munich runway, seemed – even to an unreconstructed modernist like Best – to be something other worldly, spiritual. Best recalled that night dashing down the wing in urgent pursuit of the equalising goal that would put United ahead on aggregate and take Busby to the final, that he had looked up, seen a red shirt haring into the box and crossed the ball without quite appreciating who it was. That it was the centre back who got a nosebleed if he advanced beyond the halfway line, suddenly acting as an emergency centre forward momentarily stopped him in his tracks. As Foulkes met his delicious invitation of a cross to crash the ball home, Best remembered shaking his head, as if seeking confirmation of what he had just seen: Foulkes galloping forward to score? It can't have been. But it was. Which meant surely some presiding, higher force, wishing to right previous wrongs, was in control.

So it was on 29 May 1968, just as parts of Europe were in the midst of what looked like a full-blown youth revolution, the young gallant George Best had attained the very pinnacle of the club game. He knew that – unlike Charlton – he would never get to the international summit with his country, so this was the most important evening of his playing life. And, as he so often did on a football field, in complete contrast to his off-pitch life, how he embraced the responsibility.

United were playing Benfica again. If anything, the Portuguese were even better than they had been the last time they met, and Eusebio – the player of the 1966 World Cup – was now renowned as the finest talent on the continent. But United had Best, who, even in his early 20s, was coming to be seen as the greatest Britain had yet produced, better than Matthews, better than Finney, better – certainly in his own mind – than Charlton. And that night, in United's unfamiliar change strip of royal blue, he demonstrated that there was nothing exaggerated in such a claim. With his socks gathered around his ankles, he danced across the pristine Wembley turf. He jinked, he shimmied, he dazzled. At times his ability to ride a tackle appeared to defy all known laws of gravity: surely he had to go down? In a thirty-minute spell of extra time earned after his goalkeeping colleague Alex Stepney had produced a wonder save to stop Eusebio in the act of delivering what would have been the winning goal, he scored twice. His second was a delightful dribble around the goalkeeper, rolling the ball into an empty net. It was playground football: Uninhibited, unschooled, unfettered. It was glorious.

At the final whistle, however, for once it was not photogenic Best the cameras sought. The entire focus of attention was on Busby. Everyone wanted to hug him – players, officials, spectators, and Best. Best above all wanted to hug the Boss. Everyone wanted to share his moment of catharsis. For Busby this was the ultimate vindication. The team he sent out at Wembley was made of nine home-grown players and two bought-in, exactly the same proportion as had stood in the Babes' final line up in Belgrade. He had not only done it for them, he had done it in the same way, in the fashion he had established with Edwards, Byrne and co, the mix of the dashing and the grounded, the gilded and the workaday, the creative and the industrious. He had done what he set out to do as he lay in an oxygen tent in Munich hospital: he had won it for the boys, the boys he always felt guilty about, his lost boys. And he knew something else about that victory: he had won it because he had George Best in his team. The embrace the manager gave the player in those celebratory huddles on the Wembley touchline was full of meaning.

Busby knew this was a better team even than the Babes for the simple reason it included Best. Never mind that his own time was reaching an end, never mind that he had now achieved everything he had set out to achieve, he could move on in the certain knowledge that Best was likely to be around for a lot longer yet. There was a whole lot more to come from the man around whom everything could now be constructed, the man whose skill, balance, bravery and touch would anchor United for a generation. Best would be his bequest to his successor. Best was his legacy. Best would be the heart and soul of any new side to come. After all he was only 22.

For those inclined to look beyond fond mythology, however, so reality was impinging: 'After the greatest day of my footballing life, everything is a complete blank,' Best wrote in *Blessed*. 'I don't even remember going to the official dinner. Though I'm told I was there.'

The trouble was, by now Best's own search for inner peace was becoming ever less successful. The attraction of celebrity he had so assiduously sought and then so enthusiastically embraced had long ago palled. He found it a pain that he was recognised wherever he went. He found it an intrusion that he couldn't be on his own for a moment. He was looking for the first ship off Planet Fame.

After another summer in Majorca, on his return to Manchester he took to slipping away from the mainstream, finding his own points of refuge. One was the Brown Bull pub, a rundown sleaze pit of a place on the wrong side of the railway tracks near Victoria Station. Another was Phyllis's, the after-hours drinking den in Whalley Range, run by the mother of Thin Lizzy's Phil Lynott. He was introduced to it by the Quality Street Gang, who liked to head there at the back end of a night's drinking. Increasingly, they'd find Bestie in there with them at 3 a.m. – two, three, four times a week. In part, he was going there because the appeal of being the most recognised person in any room had quickly lost its allure. But more and more he was drawn to these place for the seriousness of their drinking.

According to Michael Parkinson, Best was by now using alcohol to dull the pain of a recent discovery: having achieved everything in it, having found it ever easier, he was growing bored of the very game that had made him so renowned. He had just picked up the European Footballer of the Year for his cup-winning performances. Where else was there to go? What mountains were there left to climb? When he first played for United he had regularly got an erection as he ran out on to the Old Trafford pitch. Now, everything to do with football had gone limp. 'He got bored during the day so he drank, he was bored during the evening so he drank some more,' Parkinson wrote of his sometime drinking companion. 'Then he couldn't go home because he couldn't sleep properly, so he drank some more.'

The irony was that as Best sought escape so the arc light of celebrity followed him. Naturally enough, as Bestie became a regular, so the Brown Bull became a favoured hangout for the Manchester in-crowd, Parky included. Mike Summerbee held his stag night there; it was the only place he knew he could guarantee the presence of his best man, Best. Those who caroused there loved its earthy authenticity. While the after-hours sessions in its sticky-tiled back bar became ever more crowded, at least Best was not treated any differently from the rest. He was just one of the punters, one of the regulars, another of the alcoholics standing at the bar, shyly aloof. Hugh McIlvanney, a not infrequent participant in Brown Bull bacchanalia, noted something odd about Best in those grimy, grindsome, gritty sessions. Somehow in the maelstrom spinning around him he remained distant, not connected. He stood apart, alone, quiet and apparently detached. After watching him one night, McIlvanney wrote that Best appeared 'to have a slower psychological pulse than the rest of us'.

Michael Parkinson was another of the Best Boswells. He once chronicled a typical night that ended up at Phyllis's. 'He said goodnight to Phyllis and went outside,' Parky wrote of his drinking partner. 'It was daylight. Children were on their way to school. He went to his car and kids stopped to watch him drive away.' Drive away? Different times indeed.

Like McIlvanney, what Parky noted was the way Best had become so single-minded in his self-destruction. He stood at the bar all night, never moving, just steadily drinking. Uncomfortable as the centre of attention, his natural defence mechanism was to close down. When out on the lash, he preferred his own company. 'It's always been that way,' Best wrote in *Blessed* of an attitude that in later life saw him take up almost permanent residency in a Chelsea pub. 'And when I'm on my own I think too much. It makes it worse. I don't talk to anyone. I don't stay. I just skip from place to place until I come to my senses.'

Finally, inevitably, his after-hours life was beginning to have clear and obvious consequences on the day job. 'It's not good for an athlete to spend every afternoon fucking, every evening drinking and every morning thinking about fucking and drinking,' he once told Parky. He started to absent himself from training, claiming to be suffering from injury when he was as likely as not suffering from a hangover, or on an assignation with a woman. 'I used to go missing a lot … Miss Canada, Miss United Kingdom, Miss World,' was how he would later describe his growing absenteeism, raising an easy laugh from his fatuous ill-discipline.

He started, too, to get caught by opponents' reducers. When once he would have skipped away from a scything challenge, now he began to go down, then getting up to retaliate. Often he would seek to get his retaliation in first. And it was all, as he later admitted, a corollary of his preparation. 'The nights spent at the Brown Bull probably did more harm to me as an athlete than any other factor,' he wrote in *Blessed*. 'But I look back on them with more affection than I remember playing football. The Brown Bull recalls wonderful friendships and one hell of a lot of laughs.'

But if Best was soon slipping from the pinnacle of that Wembley triumph, he wasn't the only one. It has become enshrined in Manchester United folklore that the team that won the European Cup in 1968 was an ageing one. In fact, the average age of the team was exactly the same as one that won the club's second European Cup thirty-one years later in 1999 – and history does not recall the team of Giggs, Beckham, Neville and Butt as being one turning arthritic with age.

That glorious Wembley night, the United side had significant young talent: Brian Kidd, John Aston, David Sadler and Best himself were all 22 or younger. Alex Stepney was to go on to play for the club for another ten years. Nobby Stiles may have looked middle-aged but had only just turned 26. Indeed, only Charlton, Foulkes and Crerand could be considered to be nearing their sell-by date. But what happened after Wembley was that the collective purpose drained from the dressing room. The group urgency to deliver Busby his European Cup was sated. More to the point, his own ambition now satisfied, Busby himself had run out of energy. After the win had been secured, he made no attempt to invest in his team, to build on what had been achieved, to mend the roof while the sun shone brightest. When he could have attracted the very best talent in the world to Old Trafford, his only signing in the season that followed the win was Willie Morgan, a Best-lite. He tried to inject new life into the side by bringing through a steady flow of lads from the youth teams. But, as it turned out, these weren't worthy successors to the Babes. Carlo Sartori, Steve James, Jimmy Ryan, Francis Burns: they weren't Charlton, Stiles or Best. And Paul Edwards certainly wasn't Duncan Edwards. The old Busby certainty, that United could always refresh from its own internal resources, seemed no longer to obtain.

'Although I was not to know it at the time', Best would subsequently admit of the European Cup-winning season, 'it was the beginning of the end.'

7

Che Sera

But you've only just met her.

Sir Matt Busby

Best was right: 1968/69 was dire for United. The European champions finished eleventh in the first division. They lost the Intercontinental Cup in a violent kick fest with the Argentine side Estudiantes, during which Best was sent off for retaliation. They lost the semi-final of the European Cup to Milan, albeit after a seemingly bent referee in the Old Trafford leg of the tie turned a deliberate blind eye to what would have been a winning Denis Law shot that crossed the line by such a distance it was practically in Bolton. And, most significantly of all, they lost their leader: the by now knighted Matt Busby announced in January 1969 that he was going to step down as manager at the end of the season.

He had decided to leave on the advice of his wife Jean, who was alarmed at how exhausted he had become by the job. At the announcement of his departure there was no indication of who would be taking over that summer. Speculation about who might follow him filled the papers the rest of that season. The bookies favoured Jock Stein, Don Revie and Noel Cantwell. Brian Clough favoured himself. United had left Busby to find his own successor. And he was keeping his decision quiet.

He may have been functioning at half his potential, but still, in a fading, increasingly dispirited team, Best scored twenty-two goals in fifty-five appearances for United that year. This was the unhappy truth: the ease with which he could keep up appearances was no encouragement to knuckle down.

More and more he found himself in Busby's office, studying the wallpaper as the boss's entreaties just to keep his head down went in one ear and out the other. Best never caused a fuss. He sensed that Busby was as uncomfortable in confrontation as he was, so he meekly accepted the criticism, promising that he would sort himself out, and Busby gratefully bought the line – until it happened again. But then the manager had a difficult path to tread. Here was a player clearly grating against all the disciplines of the game, drinking far too much, not turning up for training, becoming tetchy and dissolute on the pitch. And yet even at his least engaged, he was by far the most compelling performer in a creaking, cracking, crumbling team. Busby could not risk being too hard on him. Besides, Busby saw the best in people. He thought George would come round.

There was, though, an inevitable consequence to his gentle leniency: the rest of the dressing room soon began to complain it was one rule for George another for them. Busby's solution was a simple one. George needed to settle down in his private life. Enough of the gallivanting, enough of the reckless personal endangerment. He needed to get married. That is what footballers did: they got married and the anchorage of a good woman focussed their minds; it encouraged a sense of responsibility. At their frequent meetings, the now departing manager kept telling George to find himself a wife.

In the summer of 1969, after Busby had stepped down and a new manager was about to be revealed, Best astonished everyone by doing exactly that. He announced that he had become engaged to a statuesque student named Eva Haraldsted, 21, whom he had encountered on a pre-season tour of Denmark. 'But you've only just met her,' Sir Matt is said to have spluttered.

'I am very partial to Scandinavian crumpet,' Best would later say. 'It being generally beautiful, always willing and a bit thick, so you don't have to waste time with the conversation.' It was not an attitude that suggested this was a relationship built on foundations of mutual respect. Indeed, it was short-lived. Like many an effort to make George settle down, it fell at the first hurdle. Five weeks after the announcement, Best told reporters that the engagement was off. Haraldsted returned to Copenhagen. Best added that he was too young to marry and could not promise to be faithful. His former fiancee sued for breach of promise – he used to boast he was the last man in Britain to be so sued – and she received a £500 out-of-court settlement.

One thing the promised engagement did, it finally allowed him to move on. That summer of '69 he was given permission by the club to move out of Mrs Fullaway's; the assumption was he was finally getting wed. Besides, now 23, it seemed a bit ridiculous to enforce the stay-in-digs-until-married law on the wealthiest young man about town in football. Best celebrated his new-won freedom by commissioning the architect Frazer Crane to build him a personalised gaff. He had but two stipulations: it must have a sunken bath and a snooker room. He paid £30,000 – a sizable sum in those days – for the place he christened his 'Saturn Five Space Station House' in Blossoms Lane, Bramhall, in Manchester's southern gin and Jaguar belt.

This was a pad for the times, full of swanky bachelor devices like curtains that could be closed at the touch of a button and a television that rose up electronically from a cabinet at the end of the bed. It was a James Bond lair for a modern hero. And it was called Che Sera, after the *News of the World* ran a competition for readers to come up with a name. The house-warming party was paid for by the *Daily Express*. Kenny Lynch, Tommy Trinder and the then current Misses UK and GB were all on the guest list.

This was his life now: public property. Which is what the house quickly became. It looked great on the local television news, with its big picture windows opening out on to the world outside. Instantly recognisable. A little too instantly recognisable. From the moment he moved in, there was a traffic jam on the street outside, cars reversing in his driveway, a whole convoy of sightseers fetching up daily in the hope of a glimpse of the owner. Fans started to turn up in such numbers that they would picnic on the lawn. (This didn't please his gardener, who was also the Old Trafford groundsman.) One time someone nicked all the goldfish from his pond. From the moment he moved in, he said the place made him feel like a prisoner. In the end, he only spent three nights there before he moved back to the safety of Mrs Fullaway's.

Almost as he abandoned a dream home, like everyone else he was astonished by the news emanating from Old

Trafford. The new manager at United wasn't the one any bookie predicted. No Stein, no Revie, no Clough. Just before the announcement of his appointment was made, word leaked out among club employees that Wilf McGuinness – the former player who had become reserve team coach after breaking his leg on first team duty a decade earlier – was to be made Busby's successor. And Wilf had just enough time to alert a couple of mates to put a bet on that it would be him. It was the last sound decision he made.

8

Wilf

He just agreed with you and said he'd change, he'd learned his lesson and it would be different. It never was.

Paddy Crerand

'You'd better wear a tie in the morning,' Wilf was told ahead of the announcement, like he was a schoolboy summoned before the headmaster. And in a sense he was. Nobody asked him if he wanted the job. He was just told he would do it. He salary was £80 a week. Busby had been on more than three times that.

At just 31 years old, McGuinness was a former teammate of the lads he was now managing. And he was immediately uncomfortable with the change of roles. Worse, it was soon evident to the players that he was trusted with nothing. Busby was general manager, in charge of recruitment, of transfer dealings, of everything really – still the Boss.

Busby was nearly twelve years younger than Sir Alex Ferguson was when he retired as United manager. At 60 he still had the energy to wield influence behind the scenes. At the time what he proposed seemed like a plan: he would take care of things like liaising with the board, talking to the press and transfer business, giving McGuinness the space to learn the trade. In practice it was less a plan than a recipe for distress.

Stripped of genuine authority, McGuinness was adrift from the start. He was soon failing to corral a dressing room made up of players of his own age and far greater accomplishment. In an attempt to impose himself he floundered. He introduced a blackboard and tactical lectures to those brought up on Busby's simple instruction to just go out and play. He embarrassed Bobby Charlton, he ostracised Jimmy Murphy, Willie Morgan squared up to him when he threw a hand of cards in the player's face after losing to him at poker on the way to a game. Which in turn infuriated the senior players: what was the manager doing playing cards at the back of the team bus? Eamon Dunphy put it brilliantly in *Strange Kind of Glory*, his biography of Busby: 'The torch had been passed on,' he wrote. 'Wilf grabbed the lighted end.'

His results were not propitious. In the new manager's first season he took United to eighth place in the first division; David Moyes would later be sacked for finishing seventh. Like Moyes he did steer them to a cup semi. They had arrived in the last four of the FA Cup largely thanks to Best. He was magnificent in the routing of Manchester City in the fourth round, he had scored six in the fifth-round tie at Northampton (a record he rather enjoyed rubbing in, as his friend and teammate Denis Law had once scored six in a cup tie that was abandoned due to fog, and the result was removed from the statistics).

But the semi-final replay against Leeds summed up Wilf's time in charge. Played on a Monday night at Villa Park, the manager thought it prudent that the team be billeted in a hotel in Worcester the day of the game. The idea was the players would have lunch and an afternoon nap before the pre-match tactical meeting. Bestie's idea of a snack was idiosyncratic. He spotted a woman in the hotel bar. Next thing, while all the other lads were in their rooms resting quietly, Bestie was in her room coupling noisily. Wilf knew what was going on. Incandescent, he got the hotel manager to open up the room and caught them at it. He should have banned Best there and then, disciplined him. But Best was his get out of jail card, he needed him. And Busby counselled against drama, insisting the player should be in the team. After all, how they needed him. 'He'll be fine, Wilf,' the Boss, the real boss, said.

He wasn't. Except for wretchedly failing to exploit United's most likely scoring opportunity, Best was almost entirely anonymous, his legs apparently drained of sap. Leeds would go on to win the tie after a second replay; United had missed their best chance of Wembley. In the dressing room the players were fuming. Senior pros – led by his old mate Crerand – turned on Best, berating him for his lack of professionalism. 'The trouble was he just agreed with you and said he'd change, he'd learned his lesson and it would be different,' says Crerand. 'It never was.'

In the stands, the United followers were none the wiser. They blamed Wilf for not securing a place in the final. They blamed him for Best being so sluggish. The papers too foisted blame on the manager. It was Wilf's tenure in microcosm. As for Best, he got away with it, like he always had.

The trouble was, he was sinking, and no one was throwing him a life jacket. Now in thrall to his addictions, he convinced himself they were the symptom not the cause of his malaise. For a while the two diametrically opposed job descriptions – celebrity wastrel and professional footballer – continued to run in parallel.

If Busby hoped things would improve on the pitch, he was soon disabused. In Wilf's second season United were woeful, full of holes. And Best's decline was at the centre of it all. There were endless stories in the papers about his misdemeanours. One told – in a flurry of unhappy headlines – of how he and Paddy Crerand had been arrested after an altercation at a nightclub. The short-tempered Scot had smacked someone who'd had a go at George, a fan angry at their former hero being out pissed when he should have been resting. Crerand broke the man's jaw. The cops were involved. The two United stars were charged with affray. What the papers did not know was what happened the night before Best and Crerand were due in court. George Carman, a regular at the Brown Bull, had agreed to defend the pair. The country's most celebrated barrister was confident he would get them off. As preparation for his case the QC, who enjoyed a drink almost as much as his client did, went down to the Brown Bull with Bestie. They returned to the Carman house, well oiled. As the barrister passed out on the sofa, his guest went upstairs and shagged his wife. Which may have explained Carman's faltering display in court the next day when the pair were found guilty.

That was the moral orbit Best now patrolled, one without hint of anchor. Soon after he and Crerand had been up before the beak, he punched a waitress in Ruebens nightclub and got a suspended sentence. The stories of serial infidelity and professional negligence were becoming ever more intertwined, stories that spoke of a man endlessly trying to affect an escape from who he was and what he had become.

In a pattern that was becoming familiar, faced with crisis, Best hid. Where once he'd run away from school, now he ran away from Old Trafford. The first time it happened was after he missed the train that was due to take him down to the FA's London headquarters for a disciplinary hearing. He didn't show up at Lancaster Gate and apparently disappeared. He was tracked down by the press, following a tip-off from a milkman, to the actress Sinead Cusack's flat in Islington. Within an hour of news spreading of his whereabouts, half of Fleet Street was camped outside. He spent three days trapped in the place, the rotters waiting to pounce on his departure. He was eventually released when Busby came down to rescue him, bundling him into a cab. His story was no longer being played out on the football pitch. It was unfolding on the front page of the tabloids.

'When Bestie started absconding, Matt Busby rang me and said, "where's George?" I knew of course, but I wasn't letting on,' reckoned Best's close friend, broadcaster Stuart Hall. 'So we did the contrite interview on the telly and presented him back to Matt. He apologised, said he'd change and probably meant it. The he ran away again. So then I did the second interview. Third time, he was beyond rescue.'

The thing was, Best was not without self-awareness. 'To an alcoholic lying comes as second nature,' he wrote in *Blessed*.

But it is his friend Waggy who probably comes closest to understanding what was driving Best in his self-destructive spiral. 'The fact was George liked what drink did to him,'

Waggy says. 'I tried so many times, but nothing was going to stop him. That was his tragedy. As for his attitude to women, he once said to me "nothing beats unwrapping a new sweet." Sadly, it doesn't take long to devour a sweet.'

Poor Wilf was one of those who suffered most from the collateral damage. With the man who might have made a difference now semi-detached and clearly uninterested in re-engaging, Wilf could sustain his position no longer. He was called in by Busby after a Boxing Day fixture at the Baseball Ground when United came from behind to draw 4–4 with Derby to be informed the experiment was over. But this was Manchester United, he was told, where they did things differently. He wouldn't be sacked, he could go back to his old job with the reserves, though obviously taking a pay cut on the way. Wilf tried it for a fortnight, but was too humiliated to continue and resigned. A month later, his hair fell out overnight.

'He came to United a boy and left an old man,' was the defender Tony Dunne's assessment of Wilf. He was just 33 when he walked out of Old Trafford.

9

Disenchanted

I was left struggling among players who shouldn't have been let through the front door at Old Trafford.

George Best

Busby moved back down from the directors' box into the dugout to sort things out. His first task: relocating his star player. He sent out the search parties and Best returned to training. They had a meeting and, as he always did, George said he'd knuckle down and behave. As he always did, he meant it. But this time, he did sort himself out. For a while. Filled with self-loathing, he was fed up with what he had become, fed up with waking in the morning face down on a filthy mattress in the room above the Brown Bull that was frequently his de facto lodging, fed up with the decline in his on-pitch supremacy. This time he really did get back to work, stopped drinking, trained like he used to, acted like a professional. He was doing it for the Boss, for the man he admired above all men.

Under Busby's tutelage, he was magnificent in the second half of the season, scoring fourteen goals to paper over the cracks through which McGuinness had fallen. There were still issues – he was sent off playing for Northern Ireland against Scotland in the Home Internationals that spring after throwing mud at the referee – but he gave every indication of being a man who had rediscovered his love of the game.

He returned from his summer break in Majorca looking lean, fit and ready. Photographs of him and Denis Law, stripped to the waist in pre-season training at the Cliff suggested there was no problem with his physicality. And Best liked what he encountered when he turned up for the 1971/72 season. With Busby finally deciding enough was enough, United had dispensed with the experiment of trying to promote from within. Experience was now considered the crucial quality in the man they hired to replace the great outgoing manager. They needed someone who knew his way round the block. So they brought in Frank O'Farrell, the quietly spoken Irishman who had steered Leicester City to the FA Cup final in 1969.

O'Farrell's approach to his players was of similar outlook to Busby: kindly, paternalistic, entirely non-shouty. Not that he initially needed to raise his voice. By mid November United were top of the league, driven there by Best's coruscating form. Still sober, still committed, he scored three hat-tricks that autumn as O'Farrell's new regime flourished; his goal against Sheffield United that took the Reds to the top of the table was a model of balance, skill and daring. There was a message to everyone who doubted him: boy, the Belfast Boy could still do it alright. The new manager was more than aware of where responsibility for this initial burst of success lay. He knew he had in his hands a patchy, flaky, ill-balanced team in need of significant reinvigoration. But with Best in this sort of form, his mind focussed, his trickery uncompromised, such issues appeared less pressing: the squad could be refurbished without trauma, rebuilt around the magical feet of Best. 'Every night I'd say one simple prayer: I'd thank God for George,' says O'Farrell of that time. He put

United's money where his mouth was too, raising Best's take-home unbidden, so that he became, for the first time, the highest-paid player in the club, on a basic of £250 a week – then unheard-of footballing returns. And Busby seemed more than impressed with the work the Irishman was doing: he said, as United stood at the top of the league, that O'Farrell was the best signing he had ever made.

While O'Farrell was in the ascendant, in the October of 1971, the police on Tyneside received what they thought was a credible phone call from someone purporting to be from the IRA. Best – whose old man was an Orangeman – was to be treated from now on as a legitimate target, the caller warned. Were he to play at St James's Park in the forthcoming league fixture with Newcastle, he would be shot. There were snipers out to get him. O'Farrell – kindly, considerately, decently – told Best that if he was worried, he could skip the requirement to play. Best thought it more likely the threat was made by a mischievous Geordie fan essaying an Irish accent. But the police were taking it seriously. As were United, particularly after the team bus – entirely coincidentally, it turned out – was broken into the night before the game. When they arrived at St James's Park, Best was instructed to lie on the floor of the bus. The sense of espionage was lent a comic touch when he was bundled into the ground beneath a coat.

As it happened, if the miscreant had attempted to stop Best playing through his subterfuge, it didn't work. Cajoled by the urgent need not to provide a standing target for any sniper positioned in the stands, Best never stopped running for ninety minutes, scoring the only goal of the game. Afterwards Joe Harvey, the Newcastle manager, joked that he wished someone had shot the bugger.

Clearly a false alarm, the incident nonetheless highlighted Best's fractured relationship with his homeland. As easily its most celebrated son, he was the target for every crank in the country every time he went home. The threats were routine. So he went home less and less often. The April before the Newcastle incident, he scored a hat-trick against Cyprus at Windsor Park in a European Championship qualifier, then withdrew from the Home International squad after yet another worrying threat to his life.

With the Troubles now boiling all around his rapidly deteriorating homeland, it was his parents who were on the front line. It was Dickie and Ann who were obliged to field the phone calls, who were disturbed by the threats from one side and the accusations from the other that Best was not doing enough to stand up for his brethren. It was Dickie and Ann who had to pick their way daily through the sectarian bile. And he left them to it. They never saw him now and he ignored their increasing vulnerability. He never even asked if they might wish to come to England to be near him. As he always did with a problem, he ignored it and hoped it might go away.

There was one problem which was not going to go away. After reaching the top at Christmas, United fell away alarmingly. The speed of decline was precipitous. O'Farrell seemed unable to arrest the fall. It was not for want of trying. He knew he needed to work on the squad. Except for Best, everywhere he looked his playing resources were threadbare and inadequate. He reckoned Stepney was not good enough, thought Crerand slow and past it, and believed Morgan was a con man, full of swagger and bravado but contributing not much more than noise. The trouble was, Stepney, Crerand and Morgan were all golfing partners of Busby. They had his ear. When O'Farrell made his reservations about the players clear to Busby and sought funds to replace them, he was gently rebuffed. Bubsy was looking out for his boys. And in truth, O'Farrell did not indicate from those he did manage to buy in that he should be trusted with a huge transfer budget. Sure, Ian Storey-Moore came from Nottingham Forest and might have made something of a difference, but he suffered a career-curtailing injury soon after arriving in Manchester. And Martin Buchan, who was bought from Aberdeen to provide some substance at the back, would go on to prove himself of immense value. Not that Best thought much of him. He showed his disdain for the new arrival when Buchan asked for the 2p Best had borrowed off him to make a phone call to be paid back. Best – wrongly as it turned out – characterised Buchan as the most humourless of Scots incomers.

As for the forwards O'Farrell brought in, even Best would struggle to create chances for Wyn Davies and Ted MacDougall. Best grew quickly disenchanted about the new men. These were not United players. Here he was, busting his guts to keep his side afloat and this was the material he had been given to work with.

For Best, growing ever more unresponsive to the routines and rhythms of the game, here was an opportunity to legitimise his own discontent. Here was the justification to excuse the return of his personal ill-discipline. What was the point him straining every sinew if United themselves were falling apart? Why should he be the one left with the responsibility of driving the team? Why was everything now down to him? 'I think the beginning of the end for George was when the team started to break up and the pressure was on him,' is Paddy Crerand's assessment.

In Best's mind, coming second was bad enough. To finish eleventh, eighth, eighth and eighth as Manchester United did for four seasons in the first division in the hollow years after the European Cup triumph was an insult. That night at Wembley he imagined would be the first of half a dozen such occasions, that he would be within five years cradling an unparalleled trophy collection. Instead he was carrying a shabby, crumbling parody of the club that had reached the pinnacle. He had done his bit, more than his bit, playing in virtually every game across those fallow seasons, invariably the leading scorer. Now he had had enough. For him, football was worth something only if it was done properly.

In May 1972, the press and television cameras were called to an impromptu gathering on the balcony of a holiday villa in Majorca. There, amid the popping of champagne corks and the gurgling of journalistic throats, George Best declared he was retiring from football. It took the club but a fortnight to change his mind. But he returned to training clearly not interested. O'Farrell tried endless things to re-engage him, to restore the spark. He tried to discipline him. He suggested he move back in with Mrs Fullaway. He asked Paddy Crerand to look out for him, to have him stay at the family home in a bid to restore his footballing equilibrium. None of it worked. Best had reached the point of despair. 'I was left struggling among players who shouldn't have been let through the front door at Old Trafford,' he would later say, articulating his dismay.

He played no more than a dozen games that autumn, then decided to take dramatic action to save his self-respect. He again walked away, again announced his retirement. This time it would be for good, he said. The game held no fascination for him anymore. He was a businessman now and would turn his attention to his boutique interests, plough his energies into a nightclub venture in Manchester to be called Slack Alice. He had outgrown football.

10

Limbo

I've missed the game more than I thought I would.

George Best

Best was as good as his word. Avoiding the responsibility of keeping himself in shape, he partied with unswerving conviction. He was drunk for days, weeks on end. There were more notches on his bedstead than there was wood to record his statistics. He gave full expression to his growing affection for the gaming table.

At first he appeared to be right: he didn't need football. Slack Alice opened and was an overnight success. Bruce Forsyth, Jimmy Tarbuck, Mick Jagger, Eric Clapton, Brian Ferry, everyone who was anyone was spotted there when they visited Manchester. Most compelling of all, without the need to be up in time for training, Bestie was always there, deep into the night. The queue of rubbernecking punters stretched round the block. The maître d' was a Spanish waiter called Felix who was brilliant at coordinating the place, making it hum, making it feel like the very epicentre of the fashionable world.

With his diary unconstrained by football, Best was now dating women of some renown. And in some case getting engaged to them. He had a short relationship (they were never long) with Marjorie Wallace, who claimed the Miss World crown for the USA while they were apparently betrothed. What a couple they made for a time, together providing a gushing wellspring of material for the tabloids

– Bestie and his Miss World – to the point that Wallace was stripped of her title after just 104 days because the beauty contest organisers could no longer tolerate the steamy headlines. It was a relationship that would end in more headlines when Best was arrested at a London nightclub after she had filed a complaint with the police following their break-up. He found himself in the dock before Marylebone magistrates accused of stealing her mink coat, passport and some letters. The charges were later dropped.

Susan George, the actress, and Lynsey de Paul, the singer were to join his list in those days too. As he said, in a line he used constantly in the second career he would make of telling how he buggered up his first: 'I spent a lot of money on booze, birds and fast cars. The rest I just squandered.'

Notoriety, though, had financial benefits. So successful were Best and his partners – Colin Bourne and Waggy – with their Slack Alice operation, they soon opened another place called Oscars. The tills were groaning. Everything was going so well, Bestie could not see the harm in helping himself. About as professional a businessman as he had latterly been a footballer, soon he was taking hundreds out of the cash registers every night that he could put down on the Manchester roulette tables. Cash was a neat metaphor for how he conducted his life in those days: easy come, easy go, no questions asked. Rootless, feckless, without an anchor in his life, his urge to self-destruct went into overdrive.

Inevitably there were casualties. The business partners left holding the bottom line as the profits were squandered. The queue of women who assumed his honeyed words had substance. Not to mention Frank O'Farrell, left without his playing prop. And also inevitably, given their fractured haplessness, without Best, United sank. They were heading towards the unthinkable – relegation to the second division – when, in December 1972, Busby approached the ebullient coach of the Scotland national team Tommy Docherty in the directors' lounge at Selhurst Park. Out on the pitch, O'Farrell's United were being taken apart by Crystal Palace. Docherty had an inkling what the United general manager might have in mind. Once the new man had expressed an interest in taking on the role – that's one way of putting it, Docherty later recalled that his insides did cartwheels the moment Busby raised the possibility – O'Farrell was summoned to Old Trafford for a meeting the following day. It was an unseasonably warm December afternoon when he made his way across the car park. A newsman who had been tipped off that something would be happening at the club made a passing comment about it being pleasant for the time of year. 'Aye,' said O'Farrell. 'It's a nice day for an execution.'

When Docherty arrived at Old Trafford Best had been in exile for several months, preferring a regime of booze, birds and the gaming table to sweaty runs and keepy-uppies. In his absence, the Doc went to immediate work refashioning the team. Able to charm the club chairman Louis Edwards into opening his chequebook, he bought in six new players, all Scots. Wisely sensing it was preferable to have the sharp-tongued winger onside, he made Morgan club captain. And the points began to accumulate. Relegation was no longer an imminent threat. For that season at least.

Best, meanwhile, found himself hospitalised with a thrombosis in his leg. It was a condition almost certainly induced by his lifestyle: a diet of the occasion canape washed down by several gallons of vodka and Coke was not the healthiest. He had by this time become used to throwing up in the toilets of Slack Alice or the Brown Bull, to empty his stomach in readiness for a further session on the sauce. Busby visited him in hospital, saw the state of him and suggested he'd be better off back at training. Best, once more fuelled by self-disgust, agreed. 'I've missed the game more than I thought I would,' he said, on his return to the Cliff. 'I'd like to think the drinking problems I had and the depressions they caused me are behind me.'

Docherty declared himself 'delighted' at the news and brought in a fitness trainer to work with the player. In the autumn of 1973, everyone – the Doc, the fitness trainer, Best himself – reckoned he was capable of returning to the United side. But as the manager must have suspected, it was the most false of new dawns. Indeed, Docherty was not without guile. By agreeing wholeheartedly to Busby's suggestion, he appeared to be doing everything he could to maintain the traditions of the club the great man had built. But the newcomer was aware drastic cauterising was required. He needed to rid the place of what he saw as its dependence on the old guard, the Busby guard. He needed to refashion it in his own image. Charlton had retired, Law he had sold on to Manchester City, and Best, well he sensed he could rely on the player's own death wish to do his work for him. No point arguing against the big Boss, just let the guy self-destruct; much easier to get rid of him after he had given him a chance. And if Best didn't crash and burn, well that would be a bonus no manager could reject. It was just he wasn't holding his breath.

Best played in twelve successive games in the autumn of 1973, scoring a couple of goals. But he looked bloated, off the pace, a depressing parody of his former self. Fans went home after an awful 3–0 defeat at QPR on New Year's Day 1974 wondering why he bothered. As for the drinking being a thing of the past, that day at Loftus Road he was clearly paying for a monumental New Year's Eve down at Slack Alice's, when the champagne fountains were in full flow. When he turned up late for a third round FA Cup tie against Plymouth four days later, his breath reeking of Alice's or Phylis's or the Brown Bull, Docherty sent him away, more disappointed than angry. He never returned. Finally, depressingly, it was over. This time he really was gone. The greatest player in the history of Manchester United was now so enslaved to alcohol he could no longer function as a professional footballer. 'George was a fantastic player,' said Docherty some years later. 'And he would have been an even better one if he'd been able to pass nightclubs the way he passed the ball.'

It may have taken another thirty-two years, but in many ways he died when he left Old Trafford in his latest sports car, half a dozen kids in parkas running alongside, hoping for an autograph. What the lads were witnessing that winter's afternoon in 1974 was a dead man driving. He was just 27 years old, younger than Eric Cantona was when he first arrived at Old Trafford 18 years later, determined finally to make his name. Because for George Best it never came back. He had scored 179 goals in 470 appearances for United – a testimony to his phenomenal ability. Anyone who saw him in a red shirt had an image seared on their brain of football genius. His pace, his control, his athleticism, his bravery: he was unimpeachable. And he knew he was gone the moment he walked out to his car. Years later, he had absolutely no coherent memory of the months that followed. He was in a downward spiral from which he never properly recovered.

Sure, there were moments for Fulham, the odd flash in America, one astonishing night for Stockport County. But even as he was putting on the occasional show, he knew he was faking it. When he scored what he later said was his greatest goal for San Jose Earthquakes, weaving through the defence time and again, teasing them, playing with them before tucking the ball home, he said afterwards that almost immediately the thought had crossed his mind: what if I'd just done that for Manchester United?

He knew this wasn't the real thing. And he was right. Nothing he did after he left ever touched for a moment what he had achieved at Old Trafford. Belfast's city fathers did not name their airport after him because of what he did for LA Aztecs. One hundred thousand mourners did not line the streets of Belfast to watch his funeral cortege pass by in December 2005 because of his appearance on *Wogan*. Thousands of Manchester United fans did not light up their mobile phones to form an immense spontaneous tableau during a match that coincided with the tenth anniversary of his death for the insights he gave on Sky's *Gillette Soccer Saturday* in his latter days. They did it for what he did in his prime, for the blaze of glory he seared on the greensward, for the unparalleled, unmatched, unquestionable genius he displayed. That was what made George Best great. That was what they were remembering. Everything that followed – the divorces, the domestic violence, the public drunkenness, the bullying of his only son, the bankruptcies, the sordid financial exploitation of his notoriety, the inability to stop drinking even when to continue to do so threatened his very life – was all but a sorry postscript.

He spent the thirty-one years after he left Old Trafford in an odd state of limbo, forever failing to find direction or purpose or anchor, a life lived in airport transit lounges and hotel rooms. Bestie seemed to be a spectator to his own decline, watching himself follow his mother, who drank herself to death in 1978, as if he were incapable of intervening. He couldn't even put aside the booze when he had a liver transplant, drink precipitating his death at the tragically early age of 59.

But even as he sank towards the inevitable, he never expressed any regret. Bestie may never have mourned what was squandered in those lost years, what was thrown away by his wilful inability to steer clear of booze for more than twenty minutes. But the rest of us sure did. Nothing else he achieved added up to a second of his time at United. But what he did there was significant enough to mark him out: George Best really was a giant of our national game.

Timeline

1946	22 May: Born in Belfast, to Dickie and Ann, the third of six children.
1961	Signs for Manchester United.
1963	14 September: Turns professional. Makes first team debut v. West Bromwich Albion.
1965	Helps United win their first league championship in eight years.
1966	Is hailed as 'El Beatle' by the fans of the Portuguese club Benfica after he helps United to a 5–1 win at the Stadium of Light in Lisbon in a European Cup tie. He is pictured arriving back at Manchester Airport wearing an over-sized sombrero.
1967	United win the league championship.
1968	Manchester United become the first English team to win the European Cup, Best scoring in a 4–1 extra-time triumph over Benfica at Wembley. Picks up the English and European Footballer of the Year awards.
1969	Announces his engagement to Eva Haraldsted, a Danish model. Breaks off the engagement after five weeks and is sued by her for breach of contract. Settles out of court.
1970	Scores six goals in an FA Cup fifth-round tie at Northampton. Sent off playing for

	Northern Ireland against Scotland in Belfast for throwing mud at referee.
1971	Scores a hat-trick against Cyprus in Belfast. Then withdraws from the Northern Ireland squad for the Home Internationals after threats on his life purported to be from the IRA.
1972	Announces his retirement from football.
1973	Makes a short comeback after making peace with new United boss Tommy Docherty, before again retiring after Docherty loses patience with his drinking. Opens Slack Alice nightclub in Manchester, which is initially hugely successful.
1974	Plays for Jewish Guild of Johannesburg. After being fired by them for his drinking and poor timekeeping, Barry Fry, his fellow former Manchester United youth team graduate, persuades him to turn out for Dunstable Town, the club he manages, in a friendly. His cousin Gary Reid, a member of the Ulster Defence Association, is killed during rioting in East Belfast.
1975	Signs for Stockport County in a deal by which he is paid according to the size of the crowd he attracts. Makes three league appearances and scoring two goals, before becoming one of the leading lights of the newly formed North American Soccer League with the Los Angeles Aztecs.

1976	Joins Fulham, making forty-two appearances and scoring eight goals, playing alongside Rodney Marsh and Bobby Moore.
1977	Makes the last of thirty-seven international appearances for Northern Ireland against Holland in Belfast.
1978	Joins Fort Lauderdale Strikers in America, but a wrangle over his registration between the American club and Fulham leads to Fifa imposing a worldwide ban on him. Marries first wife Angie Macdonald James in Las Vegas. Ann Best dies of a heart attack brought on by alcohol dependency.
1979	Signs a pay per play deal with Hibernian. His first game attracts a crowd four times greater than the average that season. He is sacked after going on a bender with members of the French rugby team after a Five Nations international at Murrayfield.
1980	Signs for San Jose Earthquakes and begins treatment for alcoholism.
1981	Scores what he later described as his favourite goal in a 3–2 win over former club Fort Lauderdale. Son Calum Milan Best is born.
1983	Plays five times for Bournemouth before finally retiring. His picture still decorates the wall of the executive suite at Dean Court stadium.
1984	Receives a three-month prison sentence for drink-driving offence and running away

POCKET GIANTS **GEORGE BEST**

	from the scene of an accident. He serves six weeks in Ford Open Prison, but doesn't play for the football team.
1988	A testimonial organised by friends attracts 20,000 people in Belfast and raises £75,000 to help stave off bankruptcy.
1990	Causes storm of protest after appearing drunk and swearing on Terry Wogan's BBC chat show. Claims the producers plied him with drink in the green room.
1992	Goes on a nationwide theatre tour with his old Fulham teammate Rodney Marsh: Sober he is excellent value; drunk he is a liability. Every appearance is a lottery.
1993	Films a video for Manchester United with Ryan Giggs, the latest new George Best. Tells Giggs not to make the mistakes he did. Giggs doesn't and plays for United for a further twenty years.
1995	Marries Alex Pursey, an air stewardess he met on a flight.
1996	Announces he would be interested in succeeding Jack Charlton as Republic of Ireland manager. He doesn't get the job.
1998	Joins Sky Sports as a football pundit.
2000	The biographical movie Best is released, starring John Lynch. The Academy Awards panel is not alerted.
2001	Reveals he is on standby for a liver transplant.

2002	30 July: Goes into hospital for transplant. Carried out on the NHS, the operation causes newspaper controversy as some commentators wonder why public money has been spent repairing self-inflicted damage. 8 December: Awarded a Lifetime Achievement Award at the BBC Sports Personality of the Year.
2003	Announces he is selling his trophies, including the European Cup winner's medal, in order to fund the purchase of a house in Greece.
2004	Banned from driving for six months after being found over the limit. Wife Alex wins the Rear of the Year title. He calls her the 'Arsehole of the Year'. In April they are divorced.
2005	3 October: Admitted into Cromwell Hospital in London suffering from a kidney complaint, exacerbated by the side effects of immune-suppressant drugs taken to stop the rejection of his transplanted liver. 21 November: Law and Charlton visit to pay their last respects. 25 November: Dies, aged 59.
2006	Belfast City Airport renamed George Best Airport in his memory.

Further Reading

Best, Calum, *Second Best: My Dad And Me*, Corgi.

Best, George, with Roy Collins, *Blessed: the Autobiography*, Ebury Press.

Burn, Gordon, *Best and Edwards: Football, Fame and Oblivion*, Faber.

Charlton, Sir Bobby, with James Lawton, *My Manchester United Years: The Autobiography*, Headline.

Dunphy, Eamon, *A Strange Kind of Glory*, Aurum.

George Best's Soccer Annual, Pelham Books.

Hamilton, Duncan, *Immortal*, Windmill Books.

Hobin, Steve, and Tony Park, *Sons of United: A Chronicle of the Manchester United Youth Team*, Popular Side Publications.

Lovejoy, Joe, *Bestie: Portrait of a Legend*, Sidgwick & Jackson.

Schindler, Colin, *George Best and 21 Others*, Headline.

White, Jim, *Manchester United: The Biography*, Sphere.

pocket GIANTS

A series about people who changed the world –
and why they matter.

Series Editor – Tony Morris

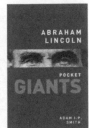